Making
MARVELOUS SCRAPBOOK PAGES

It's Easier Than You Think

We love scrapbooking! In 1996, Hot Off The Press was the very first company to develop papers exclusively for scrapbookers. Being in the retail scrapbooking market since it began has put us in a unique position to watch scrapbooking develop.

We know scrapbookers are always looking for a new look, a fresh technique or the very latest papers. **Making Marvelous Scrapbook Pages** *reflects the newest, latest and greatest developments in scrapbooking. As design leaders, we love finding new and beautiful techniques to share with our favorite people…you! And this year we're going to show you dozens of techniques so you can get the look you want on each and every page you scrap.*

While it has been exciting to see scrapbooking grow in the United States, it's also been fun to be part of it as it leaps across the "pond" and finds enthusiastic audiences in England, Australia, New Zealand, Germany and other lands. We're especially proud to present winners of our quarterly web contests (have you entered? www.paperpizazz.com). No matter where they live, these ladies are on top of the latest in scrapbooking and certainly deserve a place in this **Marvelous** *book.*

Thanks to our talented page designers. In alphabetical order, they are:

- ✿ **Tiffany Bodily**, Idaho Falls, Idaho
- ★ **Shauna Berglund-Immel** for Hot Off The Press, Inc.
- ★ **Susan Cobb** for Hot Off The Press, Inc.
- ✿ **Teri Cutts**, Portland, Oregon
- ★ **Lisa Garcia-Bergstedt** for Hot Off The Press, Inc.
- ★ **LeNae Gerig** for Hot Off The Press, Inc.
- ★ **Amy Gustafson** for Hot Off The Press, Inc.
- ✿ **Nicola Howard**, Pukekohem, New Zealand
- ✿ **Kimberly Llorens**, Portland, Oregon
- ★ **Arlene Peterson** for Hot Off The Press, Inc.

✿ *contest winner!*

For a color catalog of over 800 products, send $2.00 to **HOT OFF THE PRESS** INC.
1250 N.W. Third, Dept. B
Canby, OR 97013
phone 503•266•9102
fax 503•266•8749
http://www.paperpizazz.com

PRODUCTION CREDITS:

President:
★ Paulette Jarvey

Vice-President:
★ Teresa Nelson

Production Manager:
★ Lynda Hill

Editors:
★ Paulette Jarvey, Lynda Hill

Project Editor:
★ Lee Shaw

Photographer:
★ John McNally

Graphic Designers:
★ Jacie Pete
★ Joy Schaber

Digital Imagers:
★ Victoria Weber
★ Larry Seith
★ Gretchen Putman

Making
MARVELOUS
SCRAPBOOK PAGES

It's Easier Than You Think

Includes:
- 225 scrapbook pages
- contest winners
- 20 mini-classes
- 50 ideas with vellum

From the creators of:
Making Great Scrapbook Pages
Making Brilliant Scrapbook Pages
Making Terrific Scrapbook Pages

Mr. & Mrs.
Badman
1929

May you
always see
each other
through
hearts
filled with
love.

Daydream
Believer

brooke

April

2000

TABLE OF CONTENTS

MINI CLASSES...58-111

I LOVE VELLUM, BUT WHAT CAN I DO WITH IT?...112-139

PATTERNS...140-INSIDE THE BACK COVER

Same Photos, different designers

Same layout, different looks

Scrapbooking BASICS

Using stickers

It's a world of memories—a world of play—a world being captured for the future. It's the world of scrapbooking! And everything you need to know you really did learn in kindergarten! Find your scissors, gather the glue (acid-free, of course) and get out some of your favorite photos.

We start with an overview of the basic steps to build a page. We're even going to help you find more time to turn out album pages. Our designers are sharing their favorite short-cuts and wait till you see how using stickers can help your page tell its story in double-quick time.

We believe every scrapper sees the memory captured in a photo in a unique way and the story you chose to show will always be the right story. To prove this, we gave four designers the same pictures to use to create a page. Four completely different pages resulted each time. Every one beautiful…every one just right.

To help you reproduce the sample pages in this book, we've listed all the materials used. Paper Pizazz™ scrapbooking paper was used for all the pages in this book. These papers are sold in books and by the sheet. Book titles are in *italics* and the words "by the sheet" indicate if it's available separately.

With all the excitement we've packed into this book, you may be feeling just a little overwhelmed. Please remember, you don't have to do it all today. Treat this book like a present you're going to give to yourself over a period of time. Review a section. Do a page at a time and try out one of the ideas in here. Then the next time, try another. Soon you'll be on your way to filling albums with wonderful pages showing and telling the story of your world…the story of your life.

Ready? Let's scrap!

Sometimes posed, often spontaneous—a photo captures a moment of time. Use the camera as an extension of your eye to catch your perception of the occasion. You'll add more fun and interest to your photos.

Not a face anywhere but these shots tell a wonderfully tender story. Shooting extreme close-ups provide a uniquely personal perspective.

Living involves many emotions. Don't shoot only happy faces. Capture all of life!

Tilting the camera adds a light-hearted touch to photos such as the fun spirit displayed by these young shoppers.

Shooting up or shooting down gives a new perspective. It can also produce some great "fun house" effects.

Shoot black & white film occasionally. Study the importance of light and shadow. Try using it for a different effect.

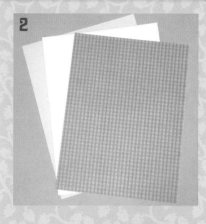

1 Select your photos based on the theme or event for your album page. You might think of each scrapbook page as having a story to tell.

2 Select plain and patterned papers to complement your photos. Choose patterned papers with colors found in your photos or that mirror the theme. Then choose solid colors to coordinate with the patterned paper. Pages 14-17 and 42-57 offer ideas for choosing and mixing papers.

3 Crop your photos to remove unimportant items (more about this on page 10). Here a plastic template helps make a perfect circle.

4 Mat your photos on plain paper (page 11 goes into more detail about matting). Glue the cropped photos to the matting paper and cut ⅛"–½" away using plain or patterned-edged scissors.

5 Arrange the photos on the background paper (pages 12–13 will offer some guidelines). Here we've mixed sizes and shapes for a pleasing arrangement.

6 Add decorative elements—Punch-Outs™, punches, stickers, die-cuts, borders, etc.

7 Finally, journal. This is where you add the words to finish your page's story. Keep it brief, or make it as complete as you think is necessary. You can journal directly on the background paper or on a separate sheet which is trimmed to fit your space.

8 Slip the completed page into a sheet protector, then into your album.

Think of it as clever cutting! Cropping allows you to focus on the important part of your photo. You can fit more cropped photos on a page, and the pages will be more interesting.

1 Trim close to the focal person, place or thing. Use straight or pattern-edged scissors.

2 Leave historical items like houses, cars, or furniture—they'll be fun to see years from now.

3 If you're hesitant about cropping older or one-of-a-kind photos, make a color copy (yes, a color copy is best even for black-and-white photos) and cut the copy for your album page.

4 Use a plastic template for smooth ovals, perfect circles and great shapes. Place the template on top of the photo and draw the shape on the photo with a pencil, then cut just inside the line. Lots of shapes are available.

5 "Silhouetting" is cutting around a person or object. This allows the focal point of the photo to stand out on your album page. Cut along the edge of the focal point, removing all the background.

6 "Bumping out" is silhouetting one area of the photo, but leaving the rest of the photo with the background. This cropping technique works especially well with clearly defined images such as the pumpkin.

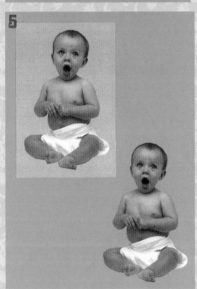

7 Don't crop Polaroid photos—if exposed, the chemicals embedded in the layers may cause deterioration of the photo and adjacent page elements. Instead cover the entire photo with a frame cropped to reveal the focal area. (Wait 10–15 minutes for freshly developed photos to dry completely before mounting.)

Matting is simply making a frame around a photo or other element with paper. Mats create a visual separation between the photos and the background paper. It helps the photo "pop" forward off the page.

1 Glue your cropped photo to a sheet of paper and cut $1/8"$–$1/2"$ away, forming a mat. Use plain paper for the mat (see the Golden Rule on page 13). Use straight-edged scissors…

2 …or pattern-edged scissors.

3 When matting a bumped-out or silhouetted photo, it's best to keep the mat simple and cut it close to the photo with straight edged scissors.

4 Double mat some photos. Varying the sizes of the mats from $1/16"$ to $1"$ wide adds interest to the page.

5 Mix using straight-edged and pattern-edged scissors on your photos and mats to add visual interest,

6 How about a triple mat just for fun? Or quadruple mat, or more?

7 Mix your mat shapes, perhaps putting an oval inside a rectangle, a circle inside a square or a heart inside a diamond.

8 Journaling on a wide mat makes good use of space and offers a great look!

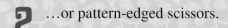

After hours of
Oh... what a catch.
Waiting... Success
At last!

1 **Establish a focal point:** The "focal point" is that element on the album page which first attracts the eye. A page without a clear focal point lacks interest. One way to create a focal point is to enlarge one photo—like the top photo in the park page at the left.

- **patterned Paper Pizazz™:** green leaf, green stripe (*Soft Florals & Patterns*)
- **solid Paper Pizazz™:** cream (*Soft Pastels*)
- **Paper Pizazz™ Cut-Outs™:** leaves (*Vellum Cut-Outs™*)
- **corkscrew scissors:** Fiskars®, Inc.
- **silver pen:** Pentel Hybrid Gel Roller
- **designer:** Arlene Peterson

2 **Vary the photo sizes:** Having one photo clearly larger than the rest adds interest to your page. The page at the left is nicely done but the large photo on the right hand page draws your attention.

- **patterned Paper Pizazz™:** pink tri dot, pink and black pattern (*Bold & Bright*)
- **solid Paper Pizazz™:** green (*Plain Pastel*); black (*Jewel Tones*)
- **1" flower and ¹⁄₂" circle punches:** Marvy® Uchida
- **jumbo lace scallop scissors:** Family Treasures, Inc.
- **black pen:** Sakura Gelly Roll
- **designer:** Arlene Peterson

3 **Vary the photo shapes:** All rectangles (or all circles or even all hearts) may make for a bland page. Change the shape of one or two photos or other elements to provide variety.

- **patterned Paper Pizazz™:** green crackled (*Spattered, Crackled, Sponged*); ivy on cream (by the sheet)
- **solid Paper Pizazz™:** tan (*Solid Jewel Tones*)
- **designer:** Arlene Peterson

4 **Overlapping elements:** Wonderful things happen when page elements touch and overlap! Not only is the viewer's eye directed from one element to another in a clear path but you can fit more or larger pieces on the page.

- **patterned Paper Pizazz™:** dog and cat party (*Annie Lang's Heartwarming Papers*)
- **solid Paper Pizazz™:** red, green, blue (*Plain Brights*)
- **Paper Pizazz Punch-Outs™:** balloons (*Annie's Kids*)
- **ripple scissors:** Fiskars®, Inc.
- **black pen:** Zig® Writer
- **designer:** Arlene Peterson

5 **Fill the center:** The center of the page attracts the eye; if it's empty, the page looks incomplete. Imagine this page without the fish. It just doesn't have lure. (We're sorry about that.)

- **patterned Paper Pizazz™:** brown plaid (*Great Outdoors*, also by the sheet)
- **solid Paper Pizazz™:** white (*Plain Pastels*); green (*Solid Jewel Tones*)
- **Paper Pizazz™ Punch-Outs™:** fish (*Vacation Punch-Outs™*)
- **wave scissors:** Fiskars®, Inc.
- **black pen:** Zig® Millenium
- **designer:** Arlene Peterson

6 Follow **"The Golden Rule"** for patterned papers. **Mat your photos on plain papers before placing them on patterned backgrounds.** A plain mat visually separates a photo from a patterned background and helps it pop off the page. On this busy pattern, the double mat was used to create even more distance.

- **patterned Paper Pizazz™:** snowflakes (*Christmas Time*, also available by the sheet)
- **solid Paper Pizazz™:** white (*Plain Pastels*); red (*Plain Brights*)
- **1¹/₂" wide, 1" wide, ¹/₂" wide snowflake punches:** Marvy® Uchida
- **1¹/₄" wide snowflake punch:** Family Treasures, Inc.
- **designer:** Arlene Peterson

So many colors and patterns and all so beautiful! How do you choose? It's easy with some simple guidelines.

#1 MATCH THE PHOTO CLOTHING

This beautiful bridesmaid and her dress put this page in the pink. Arlene chose a pink moiré paper exactly matching the dress. The bouquet Janelle is holding inspired the use of the floral vellum border and rose cut-outs. The greenery in the bouquet provided the perfect contrasting color to use for the matting and journal block. Pen work on the matting adds a delicate touch. This page can stand up with the best of them!

- **patterned Paper Pizazz™:** pink moiré (by the sheet)
- **solid Paper Pizazz™:** green (*Solid Jewel Tones*); white (*Plain Pastels*)
- **Paper Pizazz™ Cut-Outs™:** border, roses (*Lacy Vellum*)
- **corkscrew scissors:** Fiskars®, Inc.
- **decorative corner punch:** Family Treasures, Inc.
- **green pen:** Zig® Writer
- **designer:** Arlene Peterson

#1 MATCH THE PHOTO CLOTHING

It was a plaid, plaid world as soon as Arlene spotted Conner's little overalls. Although she could have used the brown and tan colors in his overalls for her papers, she found a brown plaid paper a better match. She triple matted the picture using white, plaid, an oversize brown mat and the "Golden Rule"! The torn edges of the paper, die-cut journaling, little punched ladybugs and subtle chalking make this page romp.

- **patterned Paper Pizazz™:** brown plaid (*Coordinating Colors™ Flannel Plaids*)
- **solid Paper Pizazz™:** brown (*Coordinating Colors™ Brown & White*)
- **traveler alphabet die-cuts:** Accu/Cut® Systems
- **ladybug punch:** Marvy® Uchida
- **red, brown, black decorative chalks:** Craf-T Products
- **designer:** Arlene Peterson

#2 MATCH THE PHOTO BACKGROUND

A hot day and a family swim called for a page that was wet and cool. Arlene combined a water background paper with light blue and white for a refreshingly easy page. Overlapping elements and change in photo shapes give it plenty of splash. Did you catch Arlene's trick of reversing the photo mats by putting white computer-generated journaling on light blue?

- **patterned Paper Pizazz™:** pool water (*Vacation 2*, also by the sheet)
- **solid Paper Pizazz™:** white, light blue (*Plain Pastels*)
- **wave scissors:** Fiskars®, Inc.
- **designer:** Arlene Peterson

#2 MATCH THE PHOTO BACKGROUND

'Tis the season and what better way to reflect both the photos and time of year than pine boughs background paper? The Christmas red and green solid papers make perfect matting and journal blocks, neatly capturing the clothing colors in the photos. Overlapping elements and tree punches finish wrapping up one "tree-iffic" page.

- **patterned Paper Pizazz™:** pine boughs (*Christmas*, also by the sheet)
- **solid Paper Pizazz™:** spruce green, black (*Solid Jewel Tones*); red (*Plain Brights*)
- **2¼" square with scallop edges, 1¾" square punches:** Marvy® Uchida
- **1¼" long tree punch:** Family Treasures, Inc.
- **deckle scissors:** Family Treasures, Inc.
- **black pen:** Sakura Gelly Roll
- **designer:** Arlene Peterson

#3 MATCH THE THEME

Arlene's page is the perfect summation of this very special day in Wendy's life. The grad hats and diploma patterned paper was matted on black and then positioned to the right on the red with hollow dot 12"x12" paper. (We call it "growing" a page when you use an $8^{1}/_{2}$"x11" on a 12"x12".) The red and black mats makes the grade not only with the background but with clothing colors in the photos. Varying the photo sizes and mixing the shapes of matting on Wendy's photo adds visual interest without clutter to this classy page.

- **patterned Paper Pizazz™:** grad hat/diploma (*School Days*, also by the sheet); 12"x12" red with hollow dot (*Bold & Bright*)
- **solid Paper Pizazz™:** red (*Plain Brights*); black (*Solid Jewel Tones*)
- **designer:** Arlene Peterson

#3 MATCH THE THEME

The right background papers can help tell your story. The great outdoors called Amy in this page. She began with a landscape map background paper, then quadruple matted the photo. Following the "Golden Rule", she matted it first on black, then yellow, plaid and then black again. Plaid letters cut from a template and matted on black are the perfect trail for the journaling to follow. With the paper pieced backpack, Amy leads us on an adventure making this page. The backpack pattern is on page 141.

- **patterned Paper Pizazz™:** brown plaid, landscape map (*The Great Outdoors*); brown suede (by the sheet)
- **solid Paper Pizazz™:** yellow (*Solid Muted Colors*); black (*Solid Jewel Tones*)
- **alphabet template:** Pebbles Inc.
- **black pen:** Sakura Gelly Roll
- **designer:** Amy Gustafson

#4 MATCH THE EMOTION

The flutter of nervousness a first-time mother-to-be experiences was the basis for Shauna's beautiful page. She layered a 2¹/₂" wide torn strip of sponged paper over the butterfly background paper. The photo was matted on solid white and torn plum pink vellum then offset on blue lavender vellum attached with eyelets. Gentle touches were added with the torn-edged vellum journaling block and the pastel punch-outs. A wonderful remembrance of the wonder and worry of this very special time.

- **patterned Paper Pizazz™**: butterflies (*A Woman's Scrapbook*, also available by the sheet); purple sponged (*Pretty Papers*, also by the sheet)
- **specialty Paper Pizazz™**: plum pink vellum, blue lavender vellum (*Pastel Vellum Papers*)
- **solid Paper Pizazz™**: white (*Plain Pastels*)
- **Paper Pizazz™ Punch-Outs™**: butterfly, dragonfly (*A Woman's Punch-Outs™*)
- **lavender eyelets**: American Pin/HyGlo
- **black pen**: Sakura Gelly Roll
- **designer**: Shauna Berglund-Immel

#4 MATCH THE EMOTION

Shauna put together the perfect page to show off this proud papa with his bundle of joy. The peacock feather background paper said it so well, she kept the rest of the page simple. The photo was matted on white, teal, black, yellow and black again. The journal blocks were matted on black. A fun touch was three circle punched out in teal, yellow and black, layered with an eyelet to secure them, detailed with black and white pen dots to match the "eyes" on the feathers and then strung on a white ribbon. A page to strut your stuff!

- **patterned Paper Pizazz™**: peacock feather (*Wild Things*)
- **solid Paper Pizazz™**: white, yellow (*Plain Pastels*); black, teal (*Solid Jewel Tones*)
- **¹/₂" wide and 1" wide circle punches**: Marvy® Uchida
- **white eyelets**: Stamp Studio
- **¹/₁₆" wide white satin ribbon**: Wrights®
- **black pen**: Sakura Gelly Roll
- **white pen**: Pentel Milky Gel Roller
- **designer**: Shauna Berglund-Immel

You love the sample page! BUT…your photos are nothing like those used; the colors in the sample page just won't work with the colors in your photos, it's the wrong era, season, time of day. Guess what? It's a lot easier than you may think to take the layout you love and adapt it to meet your needs! Here's how!

In this first page, LeNae creates a "sands of time" effect for these heritage photos. The page begins with a muted sandstone background paper. The pictures are matted on white trimmed with patterned-edged scissors to give the feel of old snapshots. They are then matted on a nostalgic "letters" paper, a tan or brown and completed with white. The year is journaled on a series of squares created with matting to match the photos and arranged on a "ribbon" of paper. Notice the paper banners on the photos. A lovely memory page.

- **patterned Paper Pizazz™:** letters (*Black & White Photos*, also by the sheet); sandstone (*Textured Papers*)
- **solid Paper Pizazz™:** white (*Plain Pastels*); tan, brown (*Solid Muted Colors*); black (*Solid Jewel Tones*)
  - **deckle scissors:** Family Treasures, Inc.
  - **alphabet template:** Francis Meyer, Inc.® Fat Caps
  - **white pen:** Pentel Milky Gel Roller
  - **black pen:** Zig® Millenium
  - **designer:** LeNae Gerig

Now LeNae shows how to fast forward the above layout to a bright, today kind of page. The background paper is summery with its bugs, bees and flowers, perfect for these sunshine photos. The photos are matted on white (remember the "Golden Rule"?) then on a playful check and lastly black. The bottom photo is trimmed into an oval to catch the whirling feel of the merry-go-round. Red and black ladybugs crawl whimsically in the boxes on a black matted check "ribbon". A happy, fun page.

- **patterned Paper Pizazz™:** ladybugs (by the sheet); red/black check (by the sheet); red with white dots (*Ho, Ho, Ho!!!*, also by the sheet)
- **solid Paper Pizazz™:** black (*Solid Jewel Tones*); white (*Plain Pastels*); red (*Plain Brights*)
- **1" ladybug punch:** Marvy® Uchida
- **black pen:** Zig® Millenium
- **designer:** LeNae Gerig

It's the exact same layout as those on page 18, but a sleight of LeNae's hand turns this page into a completely different story. Her choice of the blue-gray papers lend a feel of twilight as this young couple announce their engagement. The leaves in the paper support the outdoor background in the photos. Tearing the paper softens the edges of the mats while giving a gentle rustic feel. The lettering catches the effervescent joy of the moment.

- **patterned Paper Pizazz™:** blue handmade, blue handmade with leaves, tan handmade with leaves (*"Handmade" Papers*)
- **solid Paper Pizazz™:** ivory, gray (*Solid Muted Colors*)
- **deckle scissors:** Family Treasures, Inc.
- **alphabet template:** Francis Meyers, Inc.® Wacky Letters
- **white pen:** Pentel Milky Gel Roller
- **designer:** LeNae Gerig

LeNae "grows" this layout into a 12"x12" prize catch with the addition of one photo. An outdoorsy red/blue plaid complements the crackle background paper. Although all three photos are rectangles, LeNae matted each differently. Varying the width and number of the mats gives each photo a different proportion on the page. The boxes spell out the title of this story on white matted plaid squares attached to a red and blue "ribbon". Two fish Punch-Outs™ finish helping you reel in one big, beautiful page.

- **patterned Paper Pizazz™:** crackle (*Spattered, Crackled, Sponged*); red/blue plaid (*The Great Outdoors*)
- **solid Paper Pizazz™:** red, blue (*Solid Jewel Tones*); white (*Plain Pastels*)
- **Punch-Outs™:** fish (*Vacation Punch-Outs™*)
- **alphabet template:** Francis Meyer, Inc.® Fat Caps
- **black pen:** Zig® Writer
- **designer:** LeNae Gerig

It's a wonderful homespun effect Shauna creates as she shows us how to work in 4-part harmony! Placing barnwood rectangles matted on black in opposite corners makes terrific use of the border background paper. Following the "Golden Rule", red is used to pop the photos off their rustic torn-edged backgrounds. Check out Shauna's clever trick of chalking the torn edges of the mat to achieve a burnt-edge/shadow effect. This heritage page carries just the right note!

- **patterned Paper Pizazz™:** crackle (*Texture Papers*; also by the sheet); handpainted blue (*Bj's Handpainted Papers*)
- **solid Paper Pizazz™:** red, black (*Solid Jewel Tones*); white (*Plain Pastels*)
- **black decorative chalk:** Craf-T Products
- **designer:** Shauna Berglund-Immel

Shauna takes the same quadrant concept and lets it go wild on this page. Beginning with one animal print as a background, she selects three more and cuts them to fit equally in three of the page corners. Note how she places like-colored prints opposite each other to achieve balance. To separate the four papers, she uses ¹/₄" strips of black paper over the edges. All the photos and the monkey Punch-Out™ were matted identically with neutral colors. Using foam tape under the letters and the monkey's mat adds a 3-D effect. Doesn't this page just roar with possibilities!

- **patterned Paper Pizazz™:** cheetah print, rhino print, wild things letter cuts-outs (*Wild Things*); zebra print, giraffe print, leopard print and elephant print (*Wild Things*, also by the sheet)
- **solid Paper Pizazz™:** black (*Solid Jewel Tones*); white (*Plain Pastels*)
- **Paper Pizazz™ Punch-Outs™:** monkey (*Punch Art Punch-Outs™*)
- **deckle scissors:** Family Treasures, Inc.
- **foam mounting tape:** Scotch® Brand
- **white pen:** Pentel Milky Gel Roller
- **designer:** Shauna Berglund-Immel

For something soft and sweet, Shauna chose two different patterns united by a common color. Using the green stripe for the background page, she placed 6" squares of the hydrangea paper in opposite corners and used ¼" wide white stripes to make crisp edges. See how Shauna used varying photo sizes and matting to tell the story. The two individual photos are identically sized and matted. The joint photo is cropped into a heart and placed as an overlapping element. The square photo is matted to balance the journaling. It's a perfect relationship!

- **patterned Paper Pizazz™:** hydrangeas, green stripes (*Soft Florals & Patterns*)
- **solid Paper Pizazz™:** lavender (*Solid Muted Colors*); white (*Plain Pastels*)
- **scallop scissors:** Fiskars®, Inc.
- **heart template:** *Paper Flair™ Windows #2 Template*
- **foam tape:** Scotch® Brand
- **plum mist pen:** Zig® Writer
- **designer:** Shauna Berglund-Immel

It's a playful feel for this quadrant page as Shauna uses colors and patterns to join up and perform perfectly. She creates the background by placing four 3¾"x5" rectangles on a white sheet of paper leaving equal space between them and around the edge. She trims it with patterned-edged scissors and mounts it on another sheet for a quick border. Triple matting the photo with another pattern and placing it at an angle adds to the happy nature of the page. Notice Shauna used two patterns of pink and yellow papers to match the colors in Kaelin's dress. The two patterns of blue papers come from the blue ball. Three colors (plus white) and four patterns—playful indeed!

- **patterned Paper Pizazz™:** yellow dots, yellow swirls, pink dots, pink swirls, blue gingham, blue mesh (*Bright Tints*)
- **solid Paper Pizazz™:** white (*Plain Pastels*)
- **Paper Pizazz™ stickers:** girl jumping rope, ball, flowers (*Annie Lang's Little Girls*)
- **mini scallop scissors:** Fiskars®, Inc.
- **designer:** Shauna Berglund-Immel

Arlene designed a basic yet very versatile page with three papers that can be completed in jiffy time. She began this page with a 12"x12" youthful pink flower background. Using a complementary green with white dot, she cut an 8" square, matted it on white, and glued it on point centered on the background. She matted two photos on a single white mat and glued it to the center of the green dot square. $2^3/4$" green dot squares were matted on white with $1/8$" borders and placed in the corners. $1/2$" wide circle centers were glued to $1^1/4$" punched flowers. The flowers were detailed with pen before being glued in the center of each corner square. A breeze of a page!

- **patterned Paper Pizazz™:** pink floral, green with white dot, (*Mixing Soft Patterned Papers*)
- **solid Paper Pizazz™:** white (*Plain Pastels*)
- **$1^1/4$" wide flower and $1/2$" wide circle punches:** Family Treasures, Inc.
- **black pen:** Pentel Hybrid Gel Roller
- **designer:** Arlene Peterson

Keeping to her concept, Arlene began by selecting two patterned papers which pick up the blues in the photo. She cut an 8" square of marbled paper and matted it on teal before gluing it on point in the center of the swirled background. She matted three photos on teal, cropping the smaller photos so they fit beneath the large photo. The corners were created from $2^3/4$" marbled squares matted on teal with a $1^3/4$" teal square glued on point in each corner square. The journaling plaques are matted using the same papers. A retreat of sweet memories.

- **patterned Paper Pizazz™:** blue and green marble; blue and green swirl (*Great Jewel Backgrounds*)
- **solid Paper Pizazz™:** teal (*Solid Pastel Papers*)
- **designer:** Arlene Peterson

Arlene wasn't horsing around when she used her basic model on this page. (We're sorry!) She used an 8¹/₂"x11" barnwood background fitting both the theme and warm sepia tones of the photo. And what's more natural to the paddock than denim? After matting the 6¹/₂" denim square and gluing it on point, she trimmed the side points even with the edge of the paper. 2¹/₄" denim squares were matted on 2¹/₂" squares of black paper. Horse themed charms were centered on 1¹/₂" squares turned on point in the corner blocks. This page definitely belongs in the winner's circle!

- **patterned Paper Pizazz™:** barnwood, denim (*Country*, also by the sheet)
- **solid Paper Pizazz™:** black (*Solid Jewel Tones*)
- **saddle and horseshoe charms:** Creative Beginnings
- **designer:** Arlene Peterson

Arlene's page wraps itself beautifully around holiday photos. Beginning with a cheery 12"x12" red/green plaid background paper, she matted an 8" square of holly paper on white and positioned it on point. Two photos were matted on red and white and centered over the holly paper. Arlene matted two cropped photos on red and white and placed them in opposite corners. She matted 2¹/₄" white journaling plaques on 2³/₄" holly patterned papers and then on 3" white squares and glued them in the remaining corners. A gift of happy memories.

- **patterned Paper Pizazz™:** holly, Christmas plaid (*Christmas Time*, also by the sheet)
- **solid Paper Pizazz™:** white (*Plain Pastels*); red (*Plain Brights*)
- **designer:** Arlene Peterson

Sometimes a single background paper just doesn't quite say all you want it to say. Paneling is an easy technique that lets you create the perfect background without turning your pages "busy". See how our designers multiply the possibilities with some simple additions!

Amy has a terrific way to double the background paper by using panels. Here Amy found two papers ideal for a background. She matted 2"x9³/₄" strips of rubber ducky paper on blue mats with ¹/₁₆" borders. She then glued the strips evenly spaced on the bubbles paper. She matted the photos on white and blue and created white and blue journaling plaques and arranged them as shown. Two rubber ducky Punch-Outs™ finish this page we're awfully fond of!

- **patterned Paper Pizazz™:** rubber ducky, bubbles (*Baby*, also by the sheet)
- **solid Paper Pizazz™:** blue (*Baby*); white (*Plain Pastels*)
- **Paper Pizazz™ Punch-Outs:** rubber ducks (*Baby Punch-Outs™*)
- **foam mounting tape:** Scotch® Brand
- **black pen:** Sakura Gelly Roll
- **designer:** Amy Gustafson

Embellishments can be layered on panels for an additional touch without overbalancing a page. Amy began with a 12"x12" pink diamond background paper. She cut a 9"x10³/₄" piece of pink pansy paper then glued a 9" long strip of laser lace to the bottom. She cut the piece into 2¹/₄"x10³/₄" strips and matted each on ivory leaving a ¹/₁₆" border. She used gold pen to edge each panel before gluing them evenly spaced on the pink diamond background. The photos were matted on ivory and dusty pink paper and arranged with a white and pink journaling block. A tender love of a page.

- **patterned Paper Pizazz™:** pink diamonds, pink pansies (*Soft Florals & Patterns*)
- **specialty Paper Pizazz™:** laser lace (by the sheet)
- **solid Paper Pizazz™:** ivory, pink (*Solid Muted Colors*)
- **gold pen:** Sakura Gelly Roll
- **designer:** Amy Gustafson

An overall background paper, a misty "painted" paper, and photos of a long distance runner combine in a telling page. The photos were taken on a race from a mountain to the beach. Amy began with a road map background. She selected a paper of a mountain rising out of a sea of trees to represent the starting point. The paper was cut into four 2¼"x10¾" panels matted on black. They were glued ⅜" apart on the background. The photos and journaling block were matted on black and white plain papers and arranged below the mountain paper. The center photo was raised with foam tape. A first place page, Amy!

- **patterned Paper Pizazz™**: road map (*Our Vacation*, also by the sheet); mountain scene (*Great Outdoors*)
- **solid Paper Pizazz™**: white (*Plain Pastels*); black (*Solid Jewel Tones*)
- **foam mounting tape**: Scotch® Brand
- **designer**: Amy Gustafson

Panels can be dressed up to fit the occasion. When Spencer and Kaelin saw some really big presents on an outing, Amy decided to do some gift wrapping of her own. She cut 2"x7⅝" red screen panels and matted them on gold with 1/16" borders. She glued them ½" apart on green striped paper. She cut 3" squares from bright patterned papers and glued them centered 1/16" from the bottom of the gold panels. Strips of ⅜"x2" wide bright papers were cut and matted on gold before being glued as "ribbons" on the squares. Punched bows, detailed with gold pen work, were mounted with foam tape. The photos were matted on gold and white and a gift tag was made from white paper matted on gold and finished with metallic gold thread. No waiting necessary!

- **patterned Paper Pizazz™**: green striped, red screen, blue dotted, yellow gingham, and purple swirls (*Bright Tints*)
- **specialty Paper Pizazz™**: gold (*Metallic Papers*, also by the sheet)
- **solid Paper Pizazz™**: white (*Plain Pastels*)
- **1" bow punch**: McGill, Inc.
- **gift tag die-cut**: Accu/Cut® Systems
- **foam mounting tape**: Scotch® Brand
- **metallic gold thread**: Westrim® Crafts
- **black and gold pens**: Sakura Gelly Roll
- **designer**: Amy Gustafson

Our designers have to create hundreds of pages every year and always on a deadline so they each have developed little tricks to help speed along the creation of a page. While you're not under such pressure, these shortcuts can help you create more pages in less time and still have fun doing it!

LeNae Gerig: Study sample pages and try to identify all the elements. Beautifully designed pages flow together so the elements enhance without overwhelming. By careful study you will begin to develop your eye and come to recognize what to do to make your pages marvelous.

Shauna Berglund-Immel: Using Paper Pizazz™ patterned paper books is a quick way to coordinate a page. When buying patterned papers, also make sure you have complementing solid papers available. When choosing colors, stay with a warm palette or a cool palette to make coordinating papers easier. The addition of Punch-Outs™, Cut-Outs™ and stickers will provide everything needed to complete a page quickly. Always keep your scrapbooking paper and vellum stored flat or in protective covering. Store them away from heat, light and moisture.

Arlene Peterson: When looking for inspiration, spread out the papers you are considering for a page. Stand up and look at them, move them around trying different combinations. New combinations will present themselves.

Susan Cobb: Photos that focus on the person are best for scrapbooking. Give power to smaller photos by positioning them together on one mat rather than matting them individually.

Susan: To make sure your page elements are straight, stand up and look down on your work to change perspective or hold it straight in front of you at arm's length. This is especially helpful in paper quilting or collage.

LeNae: Not every page has to be exciting and innovative. Because many photos are shots of normal events in everyday life, keep several basic layouts available that can be quickly made up to accommodate these photos.

Arlene: Keep scraps. These are wonderful when used in bargello, collage, paper piecing, as journaling blocks or any time you need just a small piece of plain or patterned paper.

Shauna: Different size square punches can be used to punch quilt shapes, tea bag folding squares, letter tiles/blocks, journaling and title blocks and mosaic tiles.

Susan: An easy way to journal perfectly is to create your own tracing paper. Write your journaling on tracing paper positioned over the journal block to assure fit. Turn the tracing paper over and cover the back with pencil rubbing. Lay face up again on the journal shape and trace over the journaling with a pencil or stylus.

Susan: Use the computer to create journaling in any number of types and styles. Both plain papers and vellum papers work wonderfully with computers. Try out your journaling first on scratch paper to ensure fit and catch any errors before printing on the journaling paper. Let the printer ink dry before cutting and placing. This is especially important when using vellum papers.

Susan: When deciding how many embellishments to use on a page, an odd number usually works better than an even number. Odd looks more random. Even looks artificial (this works in flower arranging, too).

Susan: Colored transparent pens/markers may look different when used on colored papers. Try them on a scrap first.

Susan: Gel pens are opaque and the colors stay true on colored paper. Use two coats to ensure a strong color.

Arlene: When shopping for your scrapbooking supplies, also look for supplies to add interest to your page such as charms, wire, buttons, ribbon, raffia, eyelets and brads. Keep these supplies stored with your scrapbook supplies.

The beautiful part about scrapbooking is that every page is just right! Why? Because you are telling the story YOU see. To prove our point, we gave identical photos to four different designers. Every page is different and every page is just right!

MADDIE #1

LeNae took one look at Maddie in her bright little bikini and saw flower power. She chose a happy background paper echoing the colors and bubbles in the photos. She created bright flower journaling plaques matted to match the suit's print. Vellum bubbles dance between the flowers and the photos. Both are given dimension with white pen accents. This page bubbles over with fun.

- **patterned Paper Pizazz™:** yellow stripe (*A Girl's Scrapbook*)
- **specialty Paper Pizazz™:** blue vellum (*Pastel Vellum*)
- **solid Paper Pizazz™:** bright pink, melon, green, blue, red (*Plain Brights*); white (*Plain Pastels*)
- **1" wide circle punch:** Family Treasures, Inc.
- **black pen:** Sakura Gelly Roll
- **white pen:** Pentel Milky Gel Roller
- **designer:** LeNae Gerig

MADDIE #2

Shauna chose to take us to a magical realm where the moment melts into pure joy for a child lost in her bubble blowing. She selected a botanical collage paper then matted the photos on vellum, tearing the edges of some mats to tie them to the torn-edge effect in the background paper. Notice the dotted vellum mat around the larger photo also looks like bubbles. Shauna arranged the vellum bubbles so they continue out of the picture and onto the background. She matted a duplicate of the background flower on vellum and placed it to balance the page. An enchanting page.

- **patterned Paper Pizazz™:** blue/green botanical collage (*Collage Papers*)
- **specialty Paper Pizazz™:** lemon, teal, baby blue, sky blue vellum (*Pastel Vellum*); blue dot vellum (*Soft Patterns in Vellum*)
- **1" circle punch:** Family Treasures, Inc.
- **1/4" circle punch:** Marvy® Uchida
- **silver pen:** Pentel Milky Gel Roller
- **designer:** Shauna Berglund-Immel

MADDIE #3

Fun, fun, fun began to run through Amy's mind when she saw Maddie. Matching the clothing, the photos were matted on white, yellow swirl and white and the edges outlined in black. Choosing a bright pink screen paper for the background, Amy punched flowers from the bottom edge. A 3" strip of green screen paper was trimmed to look like grass and glued over the punched area. She punched flowers from the unused green and glued the pink and green flowers to the yellow-swirl die-cut letters, trimming them even with the edges. The white matted letters were glued evenly spaced on the green screen paper. After placing the journaling blocks, Amy punched "bubbles" from blue vellum and added white pen accents. A merry page, Amy!

- **patterned Paper Pizazz™:** green screen, pink screen (*Bright Tints*)
- **specialty Paper Pizazz™:** blue vellum (*Pastel Vellum Papers*)
- **solid Paper Pizazz™:** white (*Plain Pastels*)
- **1/2" circle, 1" circle, 1" flower punches:** Family Treasures, Inc.
- **2" marshmallow letter die-cuts:** Accu/Cut® Systems
- **white pen:** Pentel Milky Gel Roller
- **black pen:** Sakura Gelly Roll
- **designer:** Amy Gustafson

MADDIE #4

Tiny flowers in the background inspired Susan on this happy page. She chose a coordinating yellow stars & buttons to match both the background and Maddie's swimsuit. She cut two 10½"x2" strips of the yellow stars & buttons paper and glued them 2¼" from the top and bottom against the right side of the background. She cut a 2⅝"x9¾" strip, gluing it centered vertically 2" from the right edge. A 1"x9¾" strip was glued centered over the left end of the horizontal strips. The photos were matted on torn yellow or teal and red. 2" squares of stars & buttons paper was matted on torn papers and placed as shown. The bright flowers on Maddie's suit were captured as the perfect embellishment for our little bubble blower!

- **patterned Paper Pizazz™:** tiny red flowers on blue, stars & buttons (*Mixing Bright Papers*)
- **solid Paper Pizazz™:** red, teal (*Solid Bright Papers*); yellow (*Solid Pastel Papers*)
- **black pen:** Zig® Writer
- **designer:** Susan Cobb

SPENCER #1

Shauna shows how the right papers can make the page. She began with an elegant, masculine background. The colors blend with the photos and the gold on black border resembles roots and vines—continuing the theme of the photos. The side photos were simply matted on black. The center photo was triple matted with black and gold and raised with foam tape, making it the focal point. Vellum paper scatters gold leaves across the page and the torn edge adds to the sense of a "treasure map". So simple. So elegant. So Shauna.

- **patterned Paper Pizazz™:** gold with black border (by the sheet)
- **specialty Paper Pizazz™:** gold (*Metallic Papers*); gold leaves on vellum (*Metallic Vellum Papers*)
- **solid Paper Pizazz™:** black (*Solid Jewel Tones*)
- **foam mounting tape:** Scotch® Brand
- **gold pen:** Sakura Gelly Roll
- **black pen:** Marvy® Uchida
- **designer:** Shauna Berglund-Immel

SPENCER #2

It's flying fun on LeNae's pages as she shows off a great tip as well! What do you do when you want to do two pages but only have one sheet of the perfect paper? Do what LeNae did. She trimmed a strip off the paper, matted it and used it for a border on one page. She then matted the rest and used it for a background on the second page. Add harvest color mats, vellum leaves drifting down and they're pages you'll fall for!

- **patterned Paper Pizazz™:** watercolor fall leaves (*Watercolor Florals*); handmade green (*"Handmade" Papers*)
- **solid Paper Pizazz™:** cream (*Plain Pastels*); sage green, burnt orange, cinnamon (*Solid Jewel Colors*)
- **Paper Pizazz™ Cut-Outs™:** vellum leaves (*Vellum Cut-Outs™*)
- **black pen:** Sakura Gelly Roll
- **designer:** LeNae Gerig

SPENCER #3

Amy decided to take us right into Spencer's yard to play with him. She "built" a fence from sixteen ⅝"x4" strips of barnwood paper. The strips were placed across the top of a 12"x12" black paper, staggered slightly and leaving a narrow border of black between each. The background paper was trimmed to follow the top of the "fence line". Amy then planted the grass by trimming 3¾" off the top of a 12"x12" sheet, cutting the edge to resemble grass and matting it on black trimmed to match the edge before gluing it aligned with the bottom edge of the background paper. She cut 5¾" from the fall leaves paper, cutting around the leaves and matting the top edge with black. She placed the photos on the grass and glued the leaves paper over them with two leaves cut from the extra paper to hold the journaling plaque. A marvelous celebration of fall!

- **patterned Paper Pizazz™:** barnwood (*Country*, also by the sheet); grass, fall leaves (by the sheet)
- **solid Paper Pizazz™:** 12"x12" black (*Coordinating Colors™ Black & White*); black (*Solid Jewel Tones*); yellow (*Solid Muted Colors*)
- **designer:** Amy Gustafson

SPENCER #4

When autumn leaves began to fall, Susan gathered together a wonderful page. She matted a sheet of frosted leaves patterned paper on a sheet of fern patterned vellum, offsetting it ¼" from the top and 1½" from the right. She glued the matted sheets centered on the burgundy with leaves background 1" from the left edge. She cut an 8⅜"x3" strip of peach vellum, gluing it 2⅜" from the bottom of the frosted leaves paper. A 6½"x9½" piece of coral vellum was glued centered on the frosted leaves paper. The photos were matted on tan and burgundy papers then glued overlapping on the coral vellum paper. Gold pen was used for the journaling and to edge the vellum sheets. Susan chalked random ferns in the vellum paper with burgundy and gold chalks for a final finishing touch.

- **patterned Paper Pizazz™:** burgundy with leaves (*Mixing Jewel Patterned Papers*); frosted leaves (*Great Outdoors*, also by the sheet)
- **specialty Paper Pizazz™:** vellum fern (*Vellum Papers*); peach, coral vellum (*Pastel Vellum*)
- **burgundy, gold decorative chalks:** Craf-T
- **solid Paper Pizazz™:** burgundy (*Solid Jewel Tones*); tan (*Solid Muted Colors*)
- **gold pen:** Pentel Hybrid Gel Roller
- **designer:** Susan Cobb

SARA #1

LeNae's passion for borders lets her turn two photos into a beautiful 12"x12" album page. Beginning with a rose background, she uses pattern-edged scissors to trim off 2¹/₂". After matting the rose paper on ivory and trimming it to a ¹/₁₆" wide border, she placed it over a soft green stripe. The two photos are triple matted in the ivory and green stripe then arranged to overlap. A poetic verse is written on green vellum and two satin bows finish tying up this page. Beautifully romantic!

- **patterned Paper Pizazz™:** white roses (by the sheet); green stripe (*12"x12" Soft Tints;* also by the sheet*)
- **specialty Paper Pizazz™:** green vellum (*Pastel Vellum*)
- **solid Paper Pizazz™:** 12"x12" ivory (*Solid Pastel Papers*)
- **seagull scissors:** Fiskars®, Inc.
- **9" of ¹/₈" wide ivory satin ribbon:** C.M. Offray & Son, Inc.
- **9" of ³/₄" wide ivory satin picot ribbon:** C.M. Offray & Son, Inc.
- **white pen:** Pentel Milky Gel Roller
- **designer:** LeNae Gerig

SARA #2

Shauna created a beautiful still life for this wedding page. She started with a lacy background paper that repeats the pattern in Sara's dress. Then cutting elements from floral papers, she recreated the bouquet and finished it with tiny satin roses. Since two of the photos were shot at a distance, Shauna decided to crop away everything but the couple, making wallet-size photos. She matted these on white and then a pink vellum with gold pen edging it. The large photo she triple matted using two shades of pink vellum. Nipping out the corners with a corner punch and winding gold thread around them gives a fairy tale feeling to the photo. Dreams really do come true!

- **patterned Paper Pizazz™:** tone-on-tone white lace (*"Lace" Papers*); pink roses, white roses, ivy (by the sheet)
- **specialty Paper Pizazz™:** dark pink vellum, plum pink vellum (*Pastel Vellum Papers*)
- **Paper Pizazz™ Punch-Outs™:** gold key (*Charms Punch-Outs™*)
- **solid Paper Pizazz™:** ivory (*Plain Pastels*); green (*Solid Jewel Tones*)
- **¹/₁₆" corner hole punch:** Marvy® Uchida
- **gold metallic thread:** Westrim® Crafts
- **¹/₂" wide ivory satin roses with green leaves, ¹/₄" wide pink satin ribbon:** C.M. Offray & Son, Inc.
- **mini envelope template:** *Paper Flair™ 2 Envelopes*
- **foam mounting tape:** Scotch® Brand
- **gold pen:** Sakura Gelly Roll
- **designer:** Shauna Berglund-Immel

SARA #3

Amy chose one photo for her page—the moment when two lives have joined together with a kiss to seal the pledge. She selected a netting background paper. The photo was matted on lavender, vellum fern paper and pink vellum. She stitched the mat to the background with gold thread 3/4" from the top of page. She cut three 2¹/4" pink vellum squares and three "pressed" flower embellishments. Placing the squares over the embellishments, she stitched the edges with gold thread. Gold pen work highlights the journaling banner. A beautiful page for the moment that began a lifetime.

- **patterned Paper Pizazz™:** white netting (by the sheet); pressed flowers (*Embellishments*)
- **specialty Paper Pizazz™:** pink vellum (*Pastel Vellum*); vellum ferns (*Vellum Papers*, also by the sheet)
- **solid Paper Pizazz™:** lavender (*Solid Muted Colors*); white (*Plain Pastels*)
- **gold metallic thread:** Westrim® Crafts
- **gold pen:** Sakura Gelly Roll
- **designer:** Amy Gustafson

SARA #4

Treasured photos are tucked into this butterfly pocket on Susan's page. A 10"x10¹/2" piece of rose paper was glued centered on the pink striped background paper. She created the envelope by folding an 8¹/2"x11" sheet of vellum in half from bottom to the top. She marked 4¹/4" across the top and drew a line 4¹/2" down, cutting only on the top layer. The cut edges were folded on top and trimmed even with the envelope. Two triangles (see page 144 for pattern) of lacy floral border vellum were then glued over them. A strip of 1/4" wide silver paper was glued below the folds with the journaling written in silver pen. The photos were matted on white and silver and glued inside the envelope. Strips of 1"x2" plum vellum were folded and glued on the corners, edged by 3/8" strips of silver. A pink bow ties this memory together.

- **patterned Paper Pizazz™:** pink stripe (*Soft Florals & Patterns*); pink roses (*Soft Florals & Patterns*, also by the sheet)
- **specialty Paper Pizazz™:** plum pink vellum (*12"x12" Pastel Vellum Papers*); lacy floral border vellum (*Lacy Vellum*); metallic silver (by the sheet)
- **solid Paper Pizazz™:** white (*Solid Pastel Papers*)
- **9" of ¹/2" wide satin/sheer ribbon:** C.M. Offray & Son, Inc.
- **silver pen:** Sakura Gelly Roll
- **designer:** Susan Cobb

SHAUNA #1

Nobody holds more promise than a two year old and what better to symbolize it than butterflies? LeNae chose papers from one book to ensure perfectly matching colors and patterns. See how the green swirl repeats the motion and the purple stripe draws attention to the butterflies? Still the photo doesn't get lost because of the quadruple matting. Strips of $3/4"$ wide green swirl paper were matted on white and trimmed with pattern-edged scissors before being woven into trails for the punched and matted butterflies to flutter over. Using foam tape under the butterflies lifts them off the page into flight! A simply charming page.

- **patterned Paper Pizazz™:** butterfly, green swirl, purple stripe (*Mixing Soft Pattern Papers*)
- **solid Paper Pizazz™:** white (*12"x12" Solid Pastel Papers*); purple (*Solid Jewel Tones*)
- **$1^3/4"$ wide and $7/8"$ wide butterfly punches:** Marvy® Uchida
- **deckle and mini scallop scissors:** Fiskars®, Inc.
- **foam mounting tape:** Scotch® Brand
- **black pen:** Zig® Writer
- **designer:** LeNae Gerig

SHAUNA #2

Shauna chose childhood colors and patterns for her page. Blue gingham letters cut from a template were matted on pink and then white. Pattern-edged scissors trimmed the white into a lacy border and black pen dots gave the effect of eyelet. She punched mini-holes in the letters and tied them with embroidery floss before mounting them with glue dots. Using the same matting and pattern-edge on the bottom border, three pink buttons were tied with embroidery floss and glued over punched flowers with smaller white buttons "stitched" with the embroidery floss and glued between them. A sweet page of remembrance.

- **patterned Paper Pizazz™:** blue gingham, yellow stripe (*12"x12" Soft Tints,* also by the sheet)
- **solid Paper Pizazz™:** white, pink (*Solid Plain Pastels*)
- **$1^1/4"$ wide flower and mini-hole punches:** McGill, Inc.
- **scallop and mini-scallop scissors:** Fiskars®, Inc.
- **alphabet template:** EK Success Ltd.
- **white embroidery floss:** DMC Co.
- **four $1/2"$ wide white buttons and three $3/4"$ wide pink buttons:** Coats & Clark
- **glue dots:** Glue Dots International LLC
- **black pen:** Zig® Writer
- **designer:** Shauna Berglund-Immel

SHAUNA #3

It was peaches 'n' cream for Arlene when she created this enchanting page. She used color blocks for her mat and her background. She matted the photo on peach. She then matted four patterns on peach and glued the photo centered over it. This was then matted on cream and peach solid papers. She reversed the order of the patterns for color blocking the background. After gluing the photo to the left, she had room to add a die-cut bunny accented with pen work and chalks and a tiny bow around its neck. Choosing patterns from a coordinated collection makes mixing and matching super simple according to Arlene. You'll have your page done hippity hop with this technique.

- **patterned Paper Pizazz™:** peach/yellow plaid, yellow diamond, tulip stripe, tulip (*Mixing Soft Patterned Papers*)
- **solid Paper Pizazz™:** peach, cream (*Plain Pastels*)
- **rabbit #3 die-cut:** Accu/Cut® Systems
- **peach decorative chalk:** Craf-T Products
- **4" of 1/8" wide peach satin ribbon:** C.M. Offray & Son, Inc.
- **light brown pen:** Zig® Writer
- **designer:** Arlene Peterson

rabbit ©&™ Accu/Cut® Systems

SHAUNA #4

It's a look back through rose colored glasses for Susan in this page. She created a matted frame effect by cutting the rose stripe paper 3/8" wider on the sides and 5/8" longer top and bottom than the silver matted photo. The bold floral paper was cut 1" larger on the sides and 1 1/8" longer at the top and bottom than the photo. The stripe mat was glued to the delicate floral background paper and the bold floral glued over the stripe. Two dark pink vellum triangles were cut and edged with silver pen. They were placed at the top and bottom and the photo glued over the points centered on the background. Susan used a needle and silver thread to whip stitch the vellum to the background papers and a silver pen to complete the journaling. Triangle pattern on page 144.

- **patterned Paper Pizazz™:** rose mauve delicate floral, rose/mauve stripe, rose, mauve bold floral (*Muted Tints*)
- **specialty Paper Pizazz™:** dark pink vellum (*Pastel Vellum Papers*); metallic silver (by the sheet)
- **metallic silver thread:** Westrim® Crafts
- **silver pen:** Sakura Gelly Roll
- **designer:** Susan Cobb

So cute…so simple…so quick! That's what you'll think when you make Paper Pizazz™ stickers a part of your scrapbooking supplies. Look as our designers make marvelous pages in a flash with these clear background wonders.

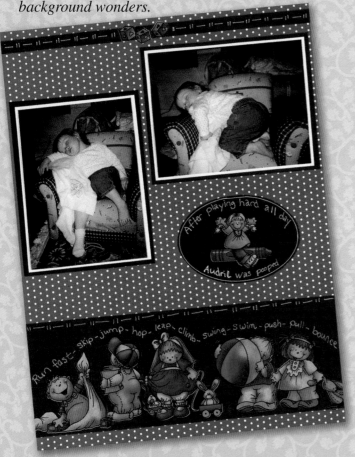

Audrie may be tired but her little friends are still having fun on this super quick page. Add *Annie Lang Toddler #2* stickers (perfect for our sleeping beauty) to the borders and journal block and you'll have a page completed in a hop, skip and jump. To make scenes bounce with life, place the figures at random—some higher, some lower, some overlapping. Kids aren't the only ones who like to play!

- **patterned Paper Pizazz™:** red with white dots (*Ho,Ho, Ho!!!*, also by the sheet)
- **solid Paper Pizazz™:** black (*Solid Jewel Tones*); white (*Plain Pastels*)
- **Paper Pizazz™ Stickers:** *Annie Lang's Toddler #2*
- **white pen:** Pentel Milky Gel Roller
- **designer:** LeNae Gerig

You won't have to hunt up a way to create a great page if you follow the bunny trail. We call this "making a scene". After matting Lauren's photo on white then spring time plaid which matches the colors of Lauren's dress, LeNae places it high on the cloud background. Cutting the grass in hills and dips and placing it slightly over the photo draws Lauren into the scene as do the overlapping bunny stickers. In no time this page becomes "egg"-stra special.

- **patterned Paper Pizazz™:** grass (by the sheet); clouds (*Vacation*, also by the sheet); pink plaid (by the sheet)
- **solid Paper Pizazz™:** white (*Plain Pastels*)
- **Paper Pizazz™ stickers:** *Ruth Ninneman's Dressed Up Bunnies*
- **black pen:** Zig® Writer
- **white pen:** Pentel Milky Gel Roller
- **designer:** LeNae Gerig

Shauna got a little "bugged" working on this page. It was perfectly put together with the background matching Jack's sweater pattern and the yellow pattern paper perfectly picking up the color. The "Golden Rule" has been obeyed when she matted and the pen work tied in the little backpack. But it needed something else. The bare center made the page look incomplete. It needed some friends to go back to school with Jack! *Annie Lang's School Time* stickers had just the friends to send along. Pick 'em, stick 'em, add some pen strokes and a bee-utiful page is done!

- **patterned Paper Pizazz™:** blue diamonds, yellow squiggles (*12"x12" Soft Tints*); yellow gingham (*12"x12" Soft Tints,* also by the sheet)
- **solid Paper Pizazz™:** white (*Plain Pastels*); red (*Plain Brights*)
- **Paper Pizazz™ stickers:** bugs with school supplies (*Annie Lang's School Time*)
- **3" circle die-cut:** Accu/ Cut® Systems
- **pinking scissors:** Fiskars®, Inc.
- **red and black pens:** Zig® Writers
- **designer:** Shauna Berglund-Immel

This page moves gracefully with the dance paper background keeping perfect step with the pink stripe. A ¹⁄₄" white strip covers any misstep in the joining. Pink swirl paper punched photo corners help our tiny dancer keep her place center stage. A "little ballerinas in their pink tutus" sticker finishes the choreography of this piece perfectly. Placed on the journaling plaque, they could tell the story even without words. Just a simple touch gets this page a standing ovation.

- **patterned Paper Pizazz™:** dance (by the sheet); pink stripe, pink swirl, green swirl (*Soft Tints*)
- **solid Paper Pizazz™:** white (*Plain Pastels*)
- **Paper Pizazz™ stickers:** ballerina stars (*Janie Dawson's Girlfriends*)
- **scalloped photo corner punch:** Marvy® Uchida
- **mini antique Victorian scissors:** Family Treasures, Inc.
- **black pen:** Sakura Gelly Roll
- **designer:** LeNae Gerig

Babies and blocks go together and Shauna really makes this page stack up. She chose a sweet baby yellow stripe for the background paper. A complementary blue dot matted on white was selected for the photo mat and for the "ribbon". Blocks were created using the stickers as the focal points. Note how the stickers tell Joshua's story with only a minimum of journaling. The rosy ribbon was matched to the cheeks of the sticker babies and finishes tying the layout together. The "Baby" sticker is the title of the sticker sheet—you can use it, too! Doesn't this page just make you smile?

oval ©Ellison® Craft & Design

- **patterned Paper Pizazz™:** yellow stripes, green swirls, blue dots (*Soft Tints*)
- **solid Paper Pizazz™:** white (*Plain Pastels*)
- **Paper Pizazz™ stickers:** *Annie Lang's Baby*
- **oval die-cut:** Ellison® Craft & Design
- **mini scallop scissors:** Fiskars®, Inc.
- **¹/₈" peach satin ribbon:** C.M. Offray & Son, Inc.
- **black pen:** Zig® Writer
- **designer:** Shauna Berglund-Immel

Celebrate how easy you can pull a page together using stickers that coordinate with your papers! Shauna chose birthday pets for her background paper. She double matted the photos and journaling blocks. A black pen stroke around the white mat gives the effect of a triple mat. The background paper was trimmed in a ripple, matted with white then backed with green for the "curtain rising" effect over the little journal blocks "hanging" from gold thread. To raise the pet stickers, Shauna placed a piece of foam tape behind each, then brushed talcum powder over the remaining sticky surface. This keeps it from sticking where you don't want it. The sticker title "Birthday" becomes the title of this page.

- **patterned Paper Pizazz™:** birthday pets (*Annie Lang's Heartwarming Papers*)
- **solid Paper Pizazz™:** red, green (*Solid Jewel Tones*); yellow (*Solid Muted Colors*); white (*Plain Pastels*)
- **Paper Pizazz™ stickers:** *Annie Lang's Birthday*
- **1" square and ¹/₁₆" hole punches:** Marvy® Uchida
- **wavy template:** EK Success Border Buddy™
- **gold metallic thread:** Westrim® Crafts
- **foam mounting tape:** Scotch® Brand
- **black pen:** Marvy® Uchida Medallion
- **designer:** Shauna Berglund-Immel

LeNae was able to match both the color and theme of the photo with a checkerboard background paper. Red and white matting for the photo and journaling blocks bounce them off the background. Dots are everywhere—in the checkerboard paper, on the white mats and in the black with white dot paper! And the bee stickers give the page a light-hearted touch. LeNae stretched the bee border sticker by cutting it into two pieces and filling the middle with another sticker. This page starts fast and finishes great!

- **patterned Paper Pizazz™:** yellow and black check (by the sheet); white dots on black (*Coordinating Colors™ Black & White*, also by the sheet)
- **solid Paper Pizazz™:** red (*Plain Brights*); white (*Plain Pastels*); black (*Solid Jewel Tones*)
- **Paper Pizazz™ stickers:** *Ruth Ninneman's Bees*
- **mini pinking scissors:** Fiskars®, Inc.
- **alphabet template:** Francis Meyer, Inc.® Fat Caps
- **black pen:** Sakura Gelly Roll
- **white pen:** Pentel Milky Gel Roller
- **foam mounting tape:** Scotch® Brand
- **designer:** LeNae Gerig

Shauna shows how to pull elements from photos and stickers to create this page! We call this interactive stickers. She starts with a wood background like the one Steven is sitting on. She chose denim and yellow mats to match the photo with denim for the letters. Now watch closely. She arranged stickers behind the letters "B" and "Y" and places the boy in the innertube swing sticker to function as the "O". She attached little green patches pen-stitched to the letters to duplicate the patch on the sticker's jeans. She runs a strand of twine from the "Y" to hold the journaling block and match the innertube sticker. Stickers become photo corners and peek playfully out from under the photo. A cute as a puppy page, Shauna!

- **patterned Paper Pizazz™:** denim, barnwood (*Country*)
- **solid Paper Pizazz™:** white (*Plain Pastels*); yellow (*Solid Muted Colors*); green (*Plain Brights*)
- **¹/₄" square punch:** McGill, Inc.
- **2" marshmallow letter die-cuts:** Accu/Cut® Systems
- **Paper Pizazz™ stickers:** *Annie Lang's Little Boys*
- **foam mounting tape:** Scotch® Brand
- **black pen:** Zig® Writer
- **designer:** Shauna Berglund-Immel

Mixing Patterned PAPERS

When you were growing up, were you taught not to mix stripes and checks…florals and plaids? Well, we have a different philosophy for scrapbooking. One of the secrets of professionally designed pages is the marvelous way patterns are mixed together without overwhelming the photos. If you love the look but you're timid about putting more than one pattern on your pages, this section will show you how to do it with confidence.

We'll show you how to "read" papers. You'll want papers whose patterns contrast. We call it "reading" light and dark, i.e., one is predominantly light and the other is "mostly" dark. You can squint or place the sheet on the floor and stand up to see if it is mostly light or dark. With that decided, you can move on to making a great page.

And wait until you see patterned paper mixing using tone-on-tone collections. Swirls, stripes, checks and florals merge into pages of charming harmony when you work with different patterned papers of the same color and tint.

Then we'll introduce you to "families" of papers. These beautiful papers share colors and pattern styles, allowing you to create an infinite number of combinations without once worrying about compatibility.

We think mixing papers is so much fun that we offer a variety of Paper Pizazz™ books full of wonderful patterns already coordinated to mix into beautiful pages. In no time at all, your pages will have the flair of designer pages.

41

Maddie loves her big sister Brittney. She wants to go everywhere with her. I hope they are always this close. July 1999.

One of the simplest tricks for mixing patterned papers is using papers from Coordinating Colors™ packets. These packs are a collection of prints and solids involving a color plus white—like the navy and white papers on this page. When mixing patterns, always use the "Golden Rule". In this page, LeNae matted the photos on plain colored papers before matting on the plaid and then matted the plaid on white before placing it on the tri-dot paper. This keeps each element sharp. On the journaling plaque, the large white space on the solid mat and the Punch-Out™ girl dominate so the effect of the plaid against the tri-dot is low-key.

- **patterned Paper Pizazz™:** navy blue plaid, navy blue tri-dot (*Coordinating Colors™ Navy & White*)
- **solid Paper Pizazz™:** navy blue, white (*Coordinating Colors™ Navy & White*)
- **Paper Pizazz™ Punch-Outs™:** *Clever Companion Punch-Outs™*
- **black pen:** Zig® Writer
- **designer:** LeNae Gerig

Arlene shows another easy way to mix patterns. Following the theme of the photo, she chose a soccer ball paper. The pattern is a large, bold black and white design. The black with white dot works wonderfully with this paper because it repeats the color and shape of the soccer ball paper but it "reads" dark while the soccer paper reads light. And of course, Arlene followed the "Golden Rule" triple matting the photo and borders. Did you notice how using the soccer ball paper in the border strips helps fill the page

- **patterned Paper Pizazz™:** soccer balls (by the sheet); black with white dot (by the sheet)
- **solid Paper Pizazz™:** white (*Plain Pastels*); black (*Solid Jewel Tones*)
- **designer:** Arlene Peterson

Joseph 1997

Susan shows how being repetitious is a great way to mix patterns. She chose a green with an overall white star pattern and a white with an overall green dot pattern. The two patterns complement each in color and design. White with green dot triangles are matted first on green and then white. The photo was matted on white and then placed with folded green paper photo corners. Green matted journaling triangles and a painted vellum sunflower embellishment neatly finish the page. Using only the two main colors for the matting, photo and journaling corners keeps this page beautifully clean and sharp.

- **patterned Paper Pizazz™:** white stars on green, green dots on white (*Hunter Green Coordinating Colors Paper Pack*)
- **solid Paper Pizazz™:** green, white (*Hunter Green Coordinating Colors Paper Pack*)
- **Paper Pizazz™ Cut-Outs™:** sunflowers (*Vellum Cut-Outs™*)
- **green pen:** Zig® Writer
- **designer:** Susan Cobb

LeNae shows another great method for mixing patterns. Inspired by the colors in Michael's golf shirt, she chose a red, white and black scheme. The white mat behind the photo makes Michael the center of attention while the red/black combinations ripple out unobtrusively. Separated by a black mat, the red with hollow dot acts as an echo of the dots in the red/black check. It is the "echo" effect that can help in choosing pattern papers. Look for papers which repeat an element of the main design, use the "Golden Rule" and you'll have a page that scores a hole in one.

- **patterned Paper Pizazz™:** red/black checks (by the sheet); red with hollow dots (by the sheet)
- **solid Paper Pizazz™:** red (*Plain Brights*); white (*Plain Pastels*)
- **ripply scissors:** McGill, Inc.
- **white pen:** Pentel Milky Gel Roller
- **designer:** LeNae Gerig

Rather than mixing patterns where a color plus white are involved, these pages show mixing tints of colors. These pages will have a color (say blue) mixed with tints of that color (like light blue). This mixing gives a different look to your pages. It all begins with the papers you choose.

Vellum is a soft, subtle way to mix patterns. LeNae chose a soft blue floral pattern for the background paper. Over this she layered blue striped vellum she chose to match the tops in the photos. The colors harmonize and the floral print peeks mistily through the vellum. Laser lace creates a feminine pocket to tuck the journaling block into. A very simple page with timeless appeal.

- **patterned Paper Pizazz™:** blue flowers (*Soft Tints*)
- **specialty Paper Pizazz™:** blue striped vellum (*Soft Patterns in Vellum*); laser lace (*Romantic Papers*, also by the sheet)
- **solid Paper Pizazz™:** white (*Plain Pastels*)
- **mini antique Victorian scissors:** Family Treasures, Inc.
- **light blue pen:** Pentel Milky Gel Roller
- **black pen:** Zig® Millenium
- **designer:** LeNae Gerig

Tone-on-tone is Susan's advice for mixing patterns. Choosing different patterns in the same colors allows for easy blending of gingham, swirls and stripes. Susan used the quadrant technique. She started with a green stripe background and then placed 5³/4" swirl and gingham squares in opposite corners with triangles of swirls and gingham in the corners. Following the "Golden Rule", ¹/4" strips of pale yellow paper cover the joining seams. A single mat on the photos and journal hearts keeps the page from getting too busy. A lovely young page.

- **patterned Paper Pizazz™:** green gingham (*12"x12" Soft Tints*); green swirls, green stripe (*12"x12" Soft Tints*, also by the sheet)
- **solid Paper Pizazz™:** pale yellow (*Solid Pastel Papers*)
- **small heart #2 die-cut:** Accu/Cut® Systems
- **black pen:** Zig® Millenium
- **designer:** Susan Cobb

heart #2 © Accu/Cut® Systems

This page just blooms with new ideas from Susan. She begins with a tone-on-tone background by placing triangles of tiny pink flower paper in the four corners creating a window over the gingham background. Then, instead of matting, she lightly chalks the edges of the triangles to blend them with the darkest shade of pink in the background. The photos are double matted using pink vellum for the second mat, keeping with the softness of the page. A pink vellum pot holds three chalked tulips, each a different pattern. As accents the tulips do not overpower this page. Bouquets to Susan for this spring beauty! Flower pot pattern on page 143.

- **patterned Paper Pizazz™:** pink gingham, pink posies (*12"x12" Soft Tints,* also by the sheet)
- **specialty Paper Pizazz™:** dark pink vellum (*Pastel Vellum*); tulips cut-outs (*Chalking Cut-Outs with Pizazz™*)
- **solid Paper Pizazz™:** pale yellow (*Plain Pastels*)
- **purple, fushia, red, orange, yellow, green decorative chalks:** Craft-T Products
- **black pen:** Zig® Millenium
- **designer:** Susan Cobb

Mixing patterns can make a simple page "beary" special…just ask Lauren's mom! LeNae chose a yellow gingham background to match the gingham in Lauren's little dress. She matted a yellow stripe on white and placed it centered on the background. The photos were matted with a pattern-edged border. LeNae then punched holes in each scallop to repeat the lace edge on the dress. Sunflowers corners were matted on yellow and other sunflowers acted as the journaling plaques. A page as adorable as its subject.

- **patterned Paper Pizazz™:** yellow stripe, yellow gingham (*Soft Tints*)
- **solid Paper Pizazz™:** white (*Plain Pastels*); yellow (*Solid Muted Colors*)
- **Paper Pizazz™ Punch-Outs™:** sunflower and daisy (*Charming Companions*)
- **seagull scissors:** Fiskars®, Inc.
- **1/8" wide hole punch:** McGill, Inc.
- **black pen:** Zig® Writer
- **designer:** LeNae Gerig

Tone-on-tone papers and paper quilting are a perfect match. Using burgundy tone-on-tone papers, Susan outlined the swirls background paper with $1/4$" wide strips of the sunburst pattern and $1/2$" wide strips of the hearts & swirls pattern. She centered a 2" wide strip of the hearts & swirls paper with pink eyelets on the page. Susan made triangles from 4" squares of striped paper cut diagonally and matted on pale pink. She cut 2" squares of the sunburst and hearts & swirls papers, cut them diagonally and reassembled the squares on the pink solid paper. Squares of 1" wide striped paper were matted on pink and topped with $1/2$" wide pink hearts. The 1" squares were placed on the 2" square and these centered over each large triangle. The photo was matted on pink solid and coral vellum and positioned offset. Pink ribbon tied through the eyelets finish this "luv" page.

- **patterned Paper Pizazz™:** burgundy swirls, burgundy stripes, burgundy sunbursts, burgundy hearts & swirls (*Jewel Tints*)
- **specialty Paper Pizazz™:** coral vellum (*Pastel Vellum Papers*)
- **solid Paper Pizazz™:** pale pink paper (*Plain Pastels*)
- **$1/2$" wide heart punch:** Marvy® Uchida
- **pink eyelets:** Stamp Studio
- **16" of $1/8$" wide pink satin ribbon:** C.M. Offray & Son, Inc.
- **black pen:** Zig® Millenium
- **designer:** Susan Cobb

Arlene created an impressionist page with the use of tone-on-tone papers. Choosing lavenders to match Hailey's jacket, she began with a crackle background paper. The white matted photo was placed on a white matted $5^3/4$"x11" rectangle of lavender spatter paper. This was fastened to the background with white eyelets. The journaling block was matted on the lavender spatter paper, white and then lavender sponged paper and white. It was attached horizontally with white eyelets. See how the choice of papers and photo is reminiscent of hazy skies, lacy leafed trees overhead and a gravel path. A perfect picnic page.

- **patterned Paper Pizazz™:** lavender crackle, lavender sponged, lavender spatter (*Muted Tints*)
- **solid Paper Pizazz™:** white (*Plain Pastels*)
- **white eyelets:** American Pin/HyGlo
- **designer:** Arlene Peterson

In August we went to Oaks Park for Grandpa's company picnic. They had a big barbecue and for dessert Hailey's favorite ice cream. She ate it right up.

Shauna shows another great technique when using tone-on-tone papers in this page. She chose colors and patterns keeping with the theme but in three different sizes or "scales". The brown grid paper "reads" almost as a solid making it an easy fit with the $3^1/2$" wide brown swirls paper matted on the right. The tiny brown diamond paper is matted on black following the "Golden Rule" forming a nice bridge between the two papers. The photo was matted on black, small brown diamonds and black again then mounted with black eyelets. Shauna bordered the page with black matted $1^3/4$" squares centered with $1^3/8$" wide stars topped with $3/4$" wide stars attached with black eyelets. She used the swirls and small diamonds paper on the black die-cut boot (note how she turned the diamonds on the side to give the effect of leather). She added a $1/4$" wide brown diamond strip matted on black, wrapped with black wire and finished with a gold charm "spur". It's the best of the west, Shauna!

- **patterned Paper Pizazz™**: black with brown swirls, brown grid, brown diamonds (*Jewel Tints*)
- **solid Paper Pizazz™**: black (*Solid Jewel Tones*); white (*Plain Pastels*)
- **$3/4$" wide and $1^3/8$" wide star, $1^3/4$" square**
- **punches:** Marvy® Uchida
- **boot #2 die-cut:** Accu/Cut® Systems
- **black eyelets:** American Pin/HyGlo
- **black 1mm wire:** Artistic Wire Ltd.
- **gold star charm:** Creative Beginnings
- **designer:** Shauna Berglund-Immel

My Heroes Have Always Been Cowboys

Daddy and Kaelin saddling up for Trick or Treating with the rest of the herd on Halloween night. Oct. 1999

Spencer and Kaelin Christmas Morning 2000

The Stockings Were Hung by the Chimney with Care...

Tone-on-tone papers are a really great way to add visual interest to a page featuring a bright and busy photo. Shauna chose a muted teal in four patterns and black as a single accent color for this Christmas page. She chose a teal diamond background and then layered teal dots, teal stripes and teal gingham in graduated rectangles on the left side of the page. Each rectangle is matted on black, separating the patterned papers. Shauna placed 1"x2" rectangles of the patterned papers on black borders along the left and bottom edges, leaving $1/16$" spaces between. By turning the stripes horizontally, Shauna gives the impression of another paper pattern. Buttons and bows, along with simple journaling blocks, complete a page that does not overwhelm the eye.

- **patterned Paper Pizazz™**: teal stripes, teal dots, teal gingham, teal diamonds (*Jewel Tints*)
- **solid Paper Pizazz™**: black (*Solid Jewel Tones*); white (*Plain Pastels*)
- **gift tag #3 die-cut:** Accu/Cut® Systems
- **$1/2$" wide black buttons:** Coats & Clark, Inc.
- **$1/8$" wide black satin ribbon:** C.M. Offray & Son, Inc.
- **black pen:** Sakura Gelly Roll
- **designer:** Shauna Berglund-Immel

The trick to this mixing technique is that both papers have the same colors used in the same shades.

Think "gardens" for a wonderful way to begin to mix floral and geometric prints. In this page, Amy picked a pink diamond and pansy print. Placed together, the diamond print becomes a trellis blooming with flowers. She cut the two papers diagonally then placed ¹/₂ of each on a 12"x12" white sheet to form the background. She trimmed 2" off the short sides of the remaining triangles, matted them on white and placed them with the patterns reversed on the background. A simple white photo mat and journal block all with broken line pen work complete the page. A tender spring moment.

- **patterned Paper Pizazz™**: pink pansies, pink diamonds (*Soft Florals & Patterns*)
- **solid Paper Pizazz™**: white (*Solid Pastel Papers*)
- **black glitter pen**: Sakura Gelly Roll
- **designer**: Amy Gustafson

A bold floral print with a plain background can work well with a tiny geometric print if selected in complementary colors. Here the black with yellow dot repeats the dominant colors in the rose on black background. The photos could easily have been overpowered by the strong background using plain mats but the geometric print keeps them in the forefront. The print also provides lift for the rose Punch-Outs™. Dark colors are a great way to create a floral page that is still "masculine". Thanks, LeNae, for making this page come up roses!

- **patterned Paper Pizazz™**: roses on black (*Watercolor Backgrounds*); black with yellow dot (*Bold & Bright*)
- **solid Paper Pizazz™**: mauve, peach (*Solid Muted Colors*); white (*Plain Pastels*)
- **Paper Pizazz™ Punch-Outs™**: roses (*Watercolor Punch-Outs™*)
- **scallop photo corner punch**: Marvy® Uchida
- **mini antique Victorian scissors**: Family Treasures, Inc.
- **black pen**: Zig® Writer
- **designer**: LeNae Gerig

In addition to selecting complementary colored floral and geometric prints, LeNae used two techniques to serve up this delectable page. Using pattern-edged scissors, she trimmed 4¼" off the rose paper and then matted it on white, repeating the pattern-edge before layering it on the striped paper. The photos were matted on white and green vellum to keep the page soft. Using the trimmed-off strip, LeNae cut out roses, placing them as photo corners and embellishments around the journaling block and on the striped paper. Foam tape lifts them off the page and adds depth. A page to suit you to a "tea".

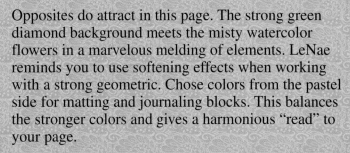

- **patterned Paper Pizazz™:** pink stripe (*Soft Florals & Patterns*); pink rose (*Soft Florals & Patterns*; also by the sheet)
- **specialty Paper Pizazz™:** green vellum (*Pastel Vellum*)
- **solid Paper Pizazz™:** 12"x12" white (*Solid Pastel Papers*)
- **seagull scissors:** Fiskars®, Inc.
- **white pen:** Pentel Milky Gel Roller
- **foam mounting tape:** Scotch® Brand
- **designer:** LeNae Gerig

Opposites do attract in this page. The strong green diamond background meets the misty watercolor flowers in a marvelous melding of elements. LeNae reminds you to use softening effects when working with a strong geometric. Chose colors from the pastel side for matting and journaling blocks. This balances the stronger colors and gives a harmonious "read" to your page.

- **patterned Paper Pizazz™:** green diamond (*Soft Tints*); purple flowers (*Watercolor Florals*)
- **solid Paper Pizazz™:** white, light green, lavender (*Plain Pastels*)
- **2½" wide giga scalloped oval punch:** Marvy® Uchida
- **mini scallop scissors:** Fiskars®, Inc.
- **black pen:** Sakura Gelly Roll
- **designer:** LeNae Gerig

Soft colors reduce the impact of a geometric design as LeNae shows with this peach check background. The white daisies and roses in the floral paper help elevate the peach roses to hold their own while the white pattern-edged matting provides a bridge between the two papers. Embellishments cut from the trimmed floral paper complete the joining of these two papers in perfect matrimony.

- **patterned Paper Pizazz™:** peach checks (*Soft Florals & Patterns*); peach roses (*Soft Florals & Patterns*, also by the sheet)
- **solid Paper Pizazz™:** 12"x12" white, ivory (*Solid Pastel Papers*)
- **2¹/₂" circle scallop giga punch:** Marvy® Uchida
- **mini antique Victorian scissors:** Fiskars®, Inc.
- **gold pen:** Pentel Metallic Gel Roller
- **designer:** LeNae Gerig

Whimsical diamonds and dots play with flowers on this light-hearted page. LeNae matted pink diamond and lavender dot papers on white before wrapping them across the hydrangea background. The coordinating colors are exactly balanced giving an even read to the layout. The heritage photo was matted on diamonds, white and purple vellum. The pastel feminine colors and airy vellum perfectly reflect the youthful laughter of the photo. A vellum journal block and lacy vellum embellishments will keep this page forever young.

- **patterned Paper Pizazz™:** lavender dots, pink diamonds, hydrangea (*Soft Florals & Patterns*)
- **specialty Paper Pizazz™:** purple vellum (*Pastel Vellum*)
- **solid Paper Pizazz™:** 12"x12" white (*Solid Pastel Papers*)
- **Paper Pizazz™ Cut-Outs™:** purple floral (*Lacy Cut-Outs™*)
- **white pen:** Pentel Milky Gel Roller
- **designer:** LeNae Gerig

Using floral and geometric papers is a great way to add a new twist to color blocking. Arlene chose the pansy paper to coordinate with the colors in the photo. The green matting neatly ties the photo to the pansy paper and is the perfect bridge from the pansy paper to the pink diamond geometric. A paper-stretching trick is to use paper which will be hidden behind other papers. Here Arlene cut the diamond mat for the photo from the background paper and then covered the hole with the matted pansy paper. She cut the embellishments from the pansy paper scraps and mounted the white matted flowers on foam tape for added dimension. A classy, classic page.

• **patterned Paper Pizazz**™: pansies, pink diamond (*Soft Florals & Patterns*)
• **solid Paper Pizazz**™: green (*Solid Jewel Tones*); white (*Plain Pastels*)
• **foam mounting tape:** Scotch® Brand
• **designer:** Arlene Peterson

Oliver, Janie and Sheryl
Spring of 1966

Isabella
18 months old

Arlene demonstrates superlative color sense in combining florals and geometrics for our little walker. She chose papers with a dark blue background matching Isabella's clothes. The pansies and coordinating stripe capture the yellows, greens, and lighter blues in the background. She cut $6^{1}/4$" wide strips of the pansy and stripe papers and glued them together to form the 12"x12" background. After matting the photo on navy blue and white, she created a mat using $3^{1}/8$"x$7^{5}/8$" strips of the stripe and pansy matted on white, navy then white again. She centered the mat over the background reversing the stripes and pansies. The cropped photo and journal block finish a page that steps out beautifully.

• **patterned Paper Pizazz**™: pansies, navy stripe (*Coordinating Florals & Patterns*)
• **solid Paper Pizazz**™: white (*Plain Pastels*); navy (*Solid Jewel Tones*)
• **designer:** Arlene Peterson

Here are 3, 4 or even 5 papers used together. Just like on page 44, the important point is that each paper uses the same shades of color as its family members.

Whoa!!! This page is beautiful but too complicated! The truth is Susan just makes it look complicated by using simple shapes and a family of papers. Didn't know papers came in families? Yup, they are related by color and design such as these papers in this page. Susan cut $1^7/8$" squares, triangles and diamond shapes from this paper family, matted them on plain brown and arranged the shapes in a "quilt" with the double matted heritage photo centered on top. If you look close, you'll see exactly how she did it. Wow work, Susan!

- **patterned Paper Pizazz™:** brown/black tiles, black chevrons on brown, muted brown diamonds (*Mixing Jewel Patterned Papers*)
- **solid Paper Pizazz™:** brown (*Solid Muted Colors*); black (*Solid Jewel Tones*)
- **black pen:** Zig® Writer
- **designer:** Susan Cobb

Susan has come up with another super technique to show off a great paper family. She starts with the sunflowers on blue diamonds as the background and adds $5^3/4$"x6" rectangles of diamonds and tiny flowers in the upper left and lower right corners. Then she cuts $1/2$" wide strips from these papers and $5/8$" wide strips of blue plaid and places them on a yellow mat in a bargello pattern (see page 80). Starting at the outer edge, glue the strips as shown working inward. Place the completed bargello in the center of your background and your matted photo centered on the bargello. Sunshine marvelous!

- **patterned Paper Pizazz™:** blue plaid, sunflowers on blue diamonds, tiny flowers on yellow plaid, green/yellow diamonds (*Mixing Soft Patterned Papers*)
- **solid Paper Pizazz™:** pale yellow (*Solid Pastel Papers*); pale green (*Solid Muted Colors*)
- **oval die-cut:** Ellison® Craft & Design
- **black pen:** Zig® Millenium
- **designer:** Susan Cobb

oval © Ellison® Craft & Design

Teri Cutts, an Honorable Mention winner in the Winter Pages with Pizazz, used a whole family of pink and yellow papers with a lavish hand in this luscious page. Teri cut ten $1/2$"x11" strips of yellow striped paper, matting four with white trimmed with pattern-edged scissors. She cut four $2^{1}/4$" squares from four different patterned papers and created a patchwork background using the yellow strips as borders. The design was framed with the white matted border strips. She layered yellow matted letters die-cut from the patterned papers over the patterned squares and added punched hearts, flowers and other embellishments throughout. Isn't this a sweetheart of a page!

- **patterned Paper Pizazz™:** yellow dot, yellow stripe, pink swirls, pink checks, pink/yellow gingham (*Soft Tints*)
- **solid Paper Pizazz™:** white (*Plain Pastels*)
- **$1/4$" heart, $3/8$" flower punches:** Family Treasures, Inc.
- **heart corner punch:** Emagination
- **vagabond letter die-cuts:** Accu/Cut® Systems
- **cloud, scallop scissors:** Fiskars®, Inc.
- **designer:** Teri Cuts

LeNae invited the whole clan to her party—florals, stripes, dots and plaids! All the papers come from the same color family of light yellow, blue and green. Practicing the "Golden Rule", she used patterned-edged scissors to trim the $1^{5}/8$"x12" floral border strips, matted them on blue trimmed with the patterned-edged scissors before gluing them to the top and bottom of the yellow plaid background paper. The photos were matted on white and blue with the couple's photo matted on a stripe before the blue. The yellow dot journaling blocks were also matted on blue. Note the use of vellum for the journal blocks. The soft translucency lifts the text without adding additional weight to the page. What a good time page, LeNae!

- **patterned Paper Pizazz™:** green floral, yellow plaid, green with yellow dots, blue stripe (*Mixing Light Patterned Papers*)
- **specialty Paper Pizazz™:** blue vellum (*Pastel Vellum Papers*)
- **solid Paper Pizazz™:** 12"x12" blue, white (*Solid Pastel Papers*)
- **$1/2$" wide heart punch:** Marvy® Uchida
- **seagull scissors:** Fiskars®, Inc.
- **mini antique Victorian scissors:** Family Treasures, Inc.
- **designer:** LeNae Gerig

How can I use thee? Let me count the ways! This might be an ode LeNae could write after showing off this family of papers. Not only do paper "families" allow you to create great individual pages, they also are perfect when you have many photos and want to keep multiple pages separate yet harmonized. LeNae offers the following advice: "Cut your paper carefully so the scraps can be used on another page. If you don't have quite enough paper to complete a "ribbon" over the background, journaling blocks can cover any gap. Using the same matting throughout further connects multiple pages." These papers have just the right relationships for every event.

- **patterned Paper Pizazz**™: navy blue/pink gingham, pansy, pink rose, purple tiles, purple diamonds, navy blue with pink stripe (*Mixing Jewel Patterned Papers*)
- **solid Paper Pizazz**™:12"x12" white, dark pink (*Solid Pastel Papers*)
- **mini antique Victorian scissors:** Family Treasures, Inc.
- **black pen:** Sakura Gelly Roll
- **designer:** LeNae Gerig

Shauna shows what happened when she introduced her family to our family of papers. She selected four patterned papers in colors of rose, green and black. She cut 3" wide strips of patterned papers and matted one long edge with a $^1/_{16}$" wide black border and then layered them horizontally on a 12"x12" pink roses background. She placed the boldest pattern at the top and worked down to the subtlest pattern at the bottom of the page. By placing the green mesh between the two main patterns, she effectively tied them together without letting the page become too busy. In creating pages with a family of patterns, it's important to keep the matting on the photos simple by using solid papers or papers that "read" as a solid like the pink-on-pink rose pattern. Two families blended beautifully.

- **patterned Paper Pizazz™**: pink roses on pink, pink paisley, green mesh, pink roses on black (*Mixing Jewel Patterned Papers*)
- **solid Paper Pizazz™**: black (*Solid Jewel Tones*)
- **$^1/_4$" wide pink satin ribbon**: C.M. Offray & Son, Inc.
- **two $^3/_4$" wide black buttons**: Coats & Clark
- **green embriodery floss**: DMC Corp.
- **foam mounting tape**: Scotch® Brand
- **black pen**: Sakura Gelly Roll
- **designer**: Shauna Berglund-Immel

Some families just bubble over with fun and so do some paper families. LeNae gathered together a spring bright collection of papers to grow this page. She cut a 4$^1/_4$"x11$^1/_4$" strip of heart checks then glued it to the right side of the 12"x12" pink background paper leaving a $^3/_8$" border. She cut a 6$^1/_2$"x9$^1/_8$" block of stars & buttons and glued it to the top left. Then she cut a 6$^1/_2$"x2$^3/_8$" block of yellow stars on blue and glued it below the yellow paper. Strips of $^1/_{16}$" wide pink were glued over the edges of the papers. The photo was matted on white, blue with yellow dots and pink with punched pink/yellow plaid corners. Punched pink hearts were matted on yellow and finished with buttons. It's always a fun event when these families gather!

- **patterned Paper Pizazz™**: heart checks, yellow stars on blue, stars & buttons, blue with yellow dots, pink/yellow plaid (*Mixing Bright Patterned Papers*)
- **solid Paper Pizazz™**: aqua blue, white, yellow (*Plain Pastels*); 12"x12" dark pink (*Solid Pastel Papers*)
- **1" and 2" wide hearts, scalloped-edged photo corner punches**: Marvy® Uchida
- **four $^3/_8$" wide clear buttons and one $^3/_4$" wide white button**: Coats & Clark
- **designer**: LeNae Gerig

Bargello (see page 80) is a fabulous way to show off a family of papers. LeNae glued ³/₄" strips of three different patterned papers to an 8¹/₄" square of goldenrod paper. She placed the square on point centered on the striped background. She then selected secondary colors of dark pink and lavender to harmonize with the paper yet provide a contrast elevating the photo off the page. Strips of ¹/₂" wide checked paper were matted on strips of ³/₄" wide lavender and placed across the corners with one strip being used as the journaling plaque. Using a family of papers in a simple design adds the richness of a more complex page while still making up quickly.

- **patterned Paper Pizazz™:** pink, floral, yellow floral with dots, pink/orange checks, pink/orange stripes (*Mixing Bright Patterned Papers*)
- **solid Paper Pizazz™:** goldenrod (*Plain Brights*); dark pink, lavender (*Plain Pastels*)
- **black pen:** Zig® Writer
- **designer:** LeNae Gerig

Baby bugs and playful posies make a big splash with Isabella on this pretty pastel page. LeNae started with a blue marble paper for the background. She tore a 3" strip from the pink with bugs paper and layered it over the left side of the background. She matted one photo on a torn blue mat, the second on lavender and torn blue mat, and the third on pink and blue with leaves. A happy little swimmer sticker was matted on lavender with ovals, blue and pink before being placed on a 3¹/₂" offset square of blue with flowers placed on point over a 3" torn lavender square. The matted sticker was glued to the center of the blue flowers paper. Little flowers stickers smile cheerily as this paper family make "sugar 'n' spice" look so nice!

- **patterned Paper Pizazz™:** blue swirl, lavender with ovals, pink lace with bugs, blue and pink leaves, blue with flowers (*Mixing Light Patterned Papers*)
- **solid Paper Pizazz™:** lavender, pink, blue (*Plain Pastels*)
- **Paper Pizazz™ stickers:** little girl swimmer, flowers (*Annie Lang's Little Girls*)
- **black pen:** Zig® Writer
- **designer:** LeNae Gerig

Susan takes this couple on a spin as she shows off these papers ability to maneuver. She cut a blue/pink sponged sheet to 8⁷/₈"x9³/₄" and matted it on pink vellum. She glued it centered on 12"x12" lavender/pink stripe with dragonflies background paper. She then cut triangles from lavender flowers and pink lace with bugs. She placed a triangle ³/₈" in from each corner, alternately colors and then placed two triangles back to back centered on each side with points extending over the corner triangles. The photo was matted on white then blue lavender vellum and glued centered over the triangles. A lovely keepsake.

- **patterned Paper Pizazz™:** lavender/pink stripes with dragonflies, lavender flowers, pink lace with bugs, blue/pink sponged (*Mixing Light Patterned Papers*)
- **specialty Paper Pizazz™:** blue lavender vellum (*12"x12" Pastel Vellum*); pink vellum (*12"x12" Pastel Vellum,* also by the sheet)
- **solid Paper Pizazz™:** white (*Plain Pastels*)
- **violet pen:** Sakura Gelly Roll
- **designer:** Susan Cobb

These ladybugs brought their whole family to this fun page beginning with a red sponged background paper matching the ladybug wings. Ladybugs romp over the yellow checked paper used for the photo mat and "ribbon". A 7¹/₄"x6¹/₂" rectangle was cut with a heart die-cut from the center and matted on black. Two 2"x1⁷/₈" strips of strips of the yellow checked paper were cut and notched on one end to look like a ribbon. These were matted on black and trimmed with patterned-edged scissors then placed on each side of the photo mat and folded back. Green with ladybug & bees paper was die-cut into letters and punched into 1³/₄" squares. The letters were matted on black and the squares matted on yellow then black. Red and black 1" wide circles formed the ladybug bodies and wings, ¹/₂" wide circles for the heads, then black wire and bead hearts antennae. Eyelet spots and black pen work add the final flourish to this cute as a bug's ear page! Place heart pattern on fold.

- **patterned Paper Pizazz™:** red sponged, yellow checked with ladybugs, green with ladybugs & bees (*Mixing Bright Patterned Papers*)
- **solid Paper Pizazz™:** black (*Solid Jewel Tones*); yellow (*Plain Pastels*)
- **1³/₄" square, 1" wide and ¹/₂" wide circle punches:** Marvy® Uchida
- **2" long marshmallow letters and heart die-cus:** Accu/Cut® Systems
- **6" length of ¹/₂" wide green satin ribbon:** C.M. Offray & Son, Inc.
- **black eyelets:** Stamp Studio
- **¹/₄" wide black heart beads:** Blue Moon Beads/ Elizabeth Ward & Co., Inc.
- **black pen:** Sakura Gelly Roll
- **designer:** Shauna Berglund-Immel

Mini CLASSES

Have you ever gotten out a magnifying glass to study a sample page trying to figure out how the designer did something? Well, put your magnifying glass away and get your calendars out because we have scheduled 20 mini-classes in the following pages.

Learn to fold tri-fold pockets, keepsake pockets, photo frames, waterfall folds and bouquet holders. You're going to love using these new nested shapes on your pages. You'll mix and match papers almost endlessly when you play with this technique! Sharpen your X-acto® knife because we're showing how to create lovely lattice borders and crisp diamond folds, then with squares, triangles, diamonds, and strips, you'll be able to create bargello and striking geometric pages. We'll help you layer up some collage, too!

Paper knots, flowers, and accessorizing pages are all on our teaching schedule. And who says pages must have square edges? Not us as our shaped pages illustrate! Interactive pages will show you how to get more photos and journaling on a page than you ever imagined. With this technique, pages become true storybooks! Borders are a great way to fill a page and help tell the story. See how to use photos to create journaling blocks in our "journaling with signs" section. And we haven't forgotten heritage photos. Beautiful colors and innovative techniques give family history a whole new look.

For many classes, there are step-by-step directions complete with illustrations to help you master the folds and cuts. Descriptions of sample pages will give you measurements and patterns so you'll be able to duplicate the effect. Then let your imagination fly!

Tri-fold pockets are a functional as well as decorative addition to an album page. They are easy to make, consisting of simple folds and gluing. Tri-fold pockets can be any size and made from plain, patterned or vellum papers. To create a tri-fold pocket:

Cut a square twice the size you want your finished pocket to be, 8" is a nice size. If using patterned paper, place the white side up.

Beginning at the bottom, fold up the cuff $1/2$"–1" and crease.

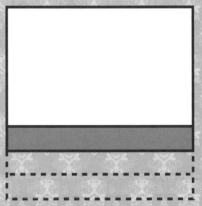

Fold up the cuff a second time the same width and crease.

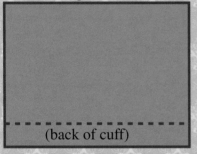

(back of cuff)

Turn the paper over so the cuff is face down and at the bottom.

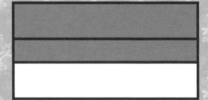

Fold the bottom of the square up until the top edge of the cuff is in the middle of the remaining square forming a pocket.

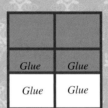

Glue | Glue
Glue | Glue

Turn the pocket over and fold both sides until they meet in the middle of the back. Glue in place. Turn the pocket over and glue to the page.

See how "charming" a tri-fold pocket can be? Arlene mixed up a wonderful page of pink florals and geometrics separated by a coordinating green. The journaling block was the perfect complement to the photo. But the balance was off. It needed something more. Arlene folded a pocket from an 8" square of green vellum with a 1" cuff, tied a heart charm to a sheer pink ribbon and glued them to the front. The journal block was slipped into the pocket. Perfectly balanced, perfectly beautiful.

- **patterned Paper Pizazz**™: pink stripe, pink diamonds (*Soft Florals & Patterns*); pink roses (*Soft Florals & Patterns,* also by the sheet)
- **specialty Paper Pizazz**™: green vellum (*Pastel Vellum*)
- **solid Paper Pizazz**™: green (*Solid Pastel Papers*)
- **12" of ⅝" wide sheer pink ribbon:** C.M. Offray & Son, Inc.
- **¾" wide gold heart charm:** Creative Beginnings
- **designer:** Arlene Peterson

An absolutely elegant heritage page is created with a tri-fold pocket! Arlene began with a blue suede background matching Bernard's tie and Zelma's eyes. She matted 1/2" wide strips of gold and vellum dot papers on a 5 1/2" square of black bordered with 1/2" strips of gold. She placed the square on point in the center of the page. The black and gold matted photos were placed in each corner. She matted the vellum lace borders on black, gold and black then glued them in the opposite corners. Gold pen work adds a delicate embellishment. Arlene created a tri-fold pocket from an 8" square of vellum lace paper with a 1" cuff, wrapped a gold metallic ribbon around it and attached a charm like the brooch in Zelma's photo. A black matted gold journaling card is slipped in the pocket. A gentle era recaptured!

- **patterned Paper Pizazz™:** navy suede (*Heritage Papers,* also by the sheet)
- **specialty Paper Pizazz™:** specialty gold (*Metallic Papers,* also by the sheet); vellum lace border (*Vellum Papers,* also by the sheet)
- **solid Paper Pizazz™:** black (*Solid Jewel Tones*)
- **3/8" wide gold metallic ribbon:** Wrights®
- **1 1/2" wide gold charm:** Creative Beginnings
- **designer:** Arlene Peterson

A border is built with tri-fold pockets on this page. Arlene matted a 4"x12" strip of green stripe paper on a 4 1/2"x12" strip of white paper and glued it at the bottom edge of the gingham background paper. She matted two photos on white, green gingham and white again. Hearts punched from the green stripe and matted on white were arranged with a white ribbon connecting them as shown. Arlene then folded three tri-fold pockets from blue vellum. She folded one from a 6" square of paper with a 3/4" cuff and two from 4" squares with 1/2" cuffs. She created journaling tags, finishing them with punched striped hearts and white ribbon. She matted a photo on white, green stripe and white before placing it in the center pocket. A page to warm the heart.

- **patterned Paper Pizazz™:** green gingham (*Soft Tints*); green stripe, blue gingham (*Soft Tints,* also by the sheet)
- **specialty Paper Pizazz™:** blue vellum (*Pastel Vellum Papers*)
- **solid Paper Pizazz™:** white (*Plain Pastels*)
- **3/4" and 2" heart punches:** Marvy® Uchida
- **1/8" hole punch:** Fiskars®, Inc.
- **gift tag #3 die-cut:** Accu/Cut® Systems
- **1/8" white satin ribbon:** C.M. Offray & Son, Inc.
- **designer:** Arlene Peterson

Waterfall folds create a lovely cascade of paper with a few simple folds. Waterfall folds make up quickly and are so versatile, you'll find new ways to use them again and again. To make a waterfall fold:

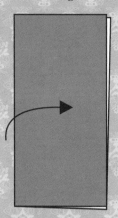

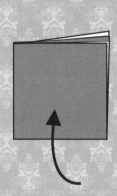

Begin with a square of paper twice the size of the finished waterfall fold you want.

Fold the paper in half.

Fold the paper again into quarters.

Turn it on point so the open edges are at the top.

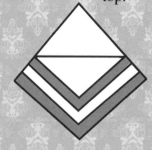

Fold down the first layer, leaving a border, and crease.

Fold down the second layer, leaving a border, and crease.

Fold down the third layer, leaving a border, and crease. Do not fold the last sheet. This way you'll have a pocket!

Waterfall folds are a natural on this lovely island page. Amy chose a magnificent background with a 12"x12" collage paper. She centered a 4"x11" strip of violet blue vellum on the page, flush with the right edge of the paper. She angled a 6½"x9" sheet of sky blue over it and a 6½"x8" sheet of turquoise blue over the sky blue. She matted the photo on silver and white. Then cutting four 2" squares of sky blue vellum, she folded each into a waterfall fold and slipped it over the photo corner. She glued the photo over the layered vellums. Silver pen work was added to the vellum sheets and the journaling was done right on the background paper. Feel that ocean breeze!

- **patterned Paper Pizazz™:** blue tropical collage (*Collage Papers*)
- **specialty Paper Pizazz™:** sky blue, turquoise blue, violet blue vellums (*Pastel Vellums*); silver (by the sheet)
- **solid Paper Pizazz™:** white (*Plain Pastels*)
- **silver pen:** Sakura Gelly Roll
- **designer:** Amy Gustafson

The combination of a very modern young woman in an old fashioned velvet hat inspired Arlene on this stunning page. She matched the clothing in the photo by choosing dark blue solid and silver papers. She placed the photo on a solid burgundy and then a blue and burgundy geometric patterned paper. Strips of $^5/_8$" burgundy feather paper were glued $^1/_4$" from the edges of the solid burgundy. Gluing 8" squares of solid blue and burgundy feather patterned papers back to back, she folded a waterfall journaling block. The 3-D effect gives wonderful depth to this page. The silver pen journaling, scrollwork, and edging on the waterfall folds create a sterling page!

- **patterned Paper Pizazz™:** burgundy/blue geometric, burgundy feather (*Mixing Jewel Patterned Papers*)
- **specialty Paper Pizazz™:** silver (*Metallic Papers*, also by the sheet)
- **solid Paper Pizazz™:** burgundy, blue (*Solid Jewel Tones*)
- **scroll work nested #3 template:** StenSource International, Inc.
- **silver pen:** Pentel Hybrid Gel Roller
- **designer:** Arlene Peterson

A tone-on-tone family of papers inspired Susan on this page with her choice of a lavender border paper for the background. She matted the photo on solid lavender leaving a $^1/_{16}$" border. She placed this centered on a $6^3/_4$"x8" piece of light lavender patterned vellum and traced around the matted photo. She cut corner to corner inside the traced area on the patterned vellum forming an "X" and folded the triangle pieces out. Susan glued a $6^1/_4$"x$7^1/_2$" dark lavender patterned vellum rectangle on the cut vellum. She folded and glued the points back over the dark lavender patterned vellum then glued the photo centered on the mat before adding photo corners. She edged a 2"x11" strip of pale lavender solid vellum with white pen and placed it $2^1/_2$" from the right side of the background paper. Susan positioned the photo over the strip and then created a waterfall journaling pocket from a 4" square of patterned vellum to hold the vellum journaling plaque. Soft colors folded into sweet memories.

- **patterned Paper Pizazz™:** lavender border paper, lavender flowered vellums (*Mixing Papers & Vellums*)
- **specialty Paper Pizazz™:** plum pink vellum (*Pastel Vellum Papers*)
- **solid Paper Pizazz™:** lavender (*Plain Pastels*)
- **silver photo corners:** Canson-Talens, Inc.
- **9" of $^1/_4$" wide white satin ribbon:** C.M. Offray & Son, Inc.
- **white pen:** Pentel Milky Gel Roller
- **designer:** Susan Cobb

Keepsake pockets are small envelopes you can fold and attach to your album pages for purely decorative purposes, or by gluing the edges, you can make them functional envelopes to hold a tiny treaure or note. To make a keepsake pocket:

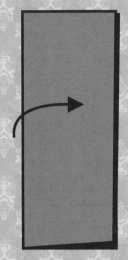

Begin with an 8¹/₂"x11" sheet.

Fold the sheet in half lengthwise white sides together

Fold the bottom of the sheet to the top, matching edges and crease.

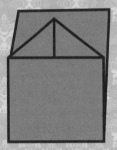

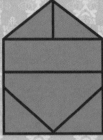

Fold the corners of the front section (two layers) to meet at the center and crease.

Fold the front down so the point is even with the bottom of the pocket.

Repeat folding the corners for the back section.

Fold the top section down, leaving a ⁵/₁₆" border.

Arlene builds sunshine into every inch of this page as she shows some tricks to unite the elements. She uses pattern-edged scissors to trim the tri-dot photo mat, the journaling ribbon and the matching strips for the envelope. All the tri-dot papers are matted on white and again on yellow with the keepsake envelope itself acting as the yellow mat. The background flowers are recreated on the embellishments from punched circles, swirls and leaves. A slat punch was used on the bottom flap creating a closure to slip the top flap through. The envelope could hold a small treasure, perhaps a pressed flower from this day. A secret garden of memories.

- **patterned Paper Pizazz™:** white with flowers, yellow tri-dot (*Lisa Williams Blue, Yellow & Green*)
- **solid Paper Pizazz™:** white, yellow (*Plain Pastels*)
- **1" circle and slat punches:** Family Treasures, Inc.
- **1" swirl and ⁷/₈" leaf punches:** Marvy® Uchida
- **scallop scissors:** Fiskars®, Inc.
- **black pen:** Sakura Gelly Roll
- **designer:** Arlene Peterson

Kim loves to help Grandma pick flowers in the garden.

Spring 2001

A vellum keepsake pocket can hold the sweetest memory in it's gossamer folds. Susan layered a 7$\frac{1}{8}$"x11" piece of lacy border vellum over a same size piece of lavender stripe paper and then placed both on the purple with bouquets background paper. The photo was matted on white and then lavender vellum and placed with silver photo corners. A keepsake pocket was folded from a second sheet of the lacy border vellum. Susan punch two holes in the flaps of the pocket and threaded a ribbon through both flaps. She tied two silver rings made from twisted silver wire to the front of the envelope with the ribbon. The ribbon can be undone to open the envelope. And the envelope is the perfect size to hold a remembrance of the dream begun on this day.

- **patterned Paper Pizazz™:** lavender/purple stripe, purple with bouquets (*Muted Tints*)
- **specialty Paper Pizazz™:** lavender vellum (*Pastel Vellum Papers*); lacy border vellum (*Lacy Vellum*)
- **solid Paper Pizazz™:** white (*Plain Pastels*)
- **$\frac{1}{8}$" hole punch:** McGill, Inc.
- **12" of 24-gauge silver plated copper wire:** Artistic Wire Ltd.
- **silver photo corners:** Canson-Talens, Inc.
- **6" of $\frac{1}{4}$" white satin ribbon:** C.M. Offray & Son, Inc.
- **silver pen:** Sakura Gelly Roll
- **designer:** Susan Cobb

Blue-on-blue is a marvelous effect in this very feminine page. Susan layered blue tone-on-tone floral vellum over a white moiré background paper. Cutting a sheet of blue vellum on the diagonal, she covered the right side adding depth to the background. The photo was matted on lavender blue solid then white with lavender blue photo corners. After gluing the photo in the center of the page, Susan folded a keepsake pocket from a sheet of blue tone-on-tone flourishes vellum and finished it with silver pen. She stitched a raised button on each fold before gluing the bottom fold to the pocket. Fused pearls were wrapped around the button to secure the pocket and it was glued under the photo. Additional fused pearls were glued over the vellum seams on both sides of the photo. A dreamy page. Susan!

- **patterned Paper Pizazz™:** white moiré (by the sheet)
- **specialty Paper Pizazz™:** blue tone-on-tone floral vellum, blue tone-on-tone flourishes vellum (*Tone-on-Tone Vellum*)
- **solid Paper Pizazz™:** lavender blue (*Solid Muted Colors*); white (*Plain Pastels*)
- **2 white raised shank buttons:** Coats & Clark
- **20" of 3mm white fused pearls:** Wrights®
- **silver pen:** Sakura Gelly Roll
- **black pen:** Zig® Millenium
- **designer:** Susan Cobb

Folded frames will be the answer to many photo problems. A folded frame can add size to smaller photos. It can crop elements from photos you don't want to cut. It protects photos you don't want to mat such as heritage photos and it can add a distinctive touch to your page. To make folded frames:

To determine the size of paper you'll need, add 2" to the length and width of your photo and cut out your frame paper.

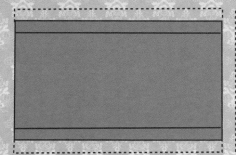

Fold the long sides in 1" on each side. Crease and unfold.

Fold the short sides in 1" on each side. Crease and unfold.

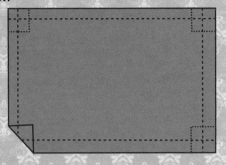

A the square was formed in each corner when the paper was folded. Fold the corner diagonally until this square is inside the fold lines. Crease. Repeat for all four corners.

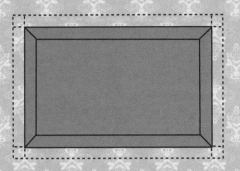

Fold each side in along the original fold lines. Glue the edges.

Folded frames can be an elegant solution to heritage pages. Beginning with 4¹/2"x6" rectangles of copper paper, Arlene trimmed an ¹/8" decorative border using pattern-edged scissors. The frames are folded and placed around the photos. The photos are matted on black with a border punched edge then matted again on gold and black. The punched-out border pieces are glued to the folded frames and echo the background paper. Copper paper journaling plaques are matted on black, gold and black again repeating the background colors. It's yesterday once more.

- **patterned Paper Pizazz™**: 12"x12" gold with black border (by the sheet)
- **specialty Paper Pizazz™**: gold, copper (*Metallic Papers*, also by the sheet)
- **solid Paper Pizazz™**: black (*Solid Jewel Tones*)
- **border punch:** McGill, Inc.
- **jumbo lace scallop scissors:** Family Treasures, Inc.
- **designer:** Arlene Peterson

A folded frame is perfect for "cropping" a photo without actually cutting it. Note the wonderful use of color and pattern in this page. Arlene used a 7"x9" piece of pink tri-dot paper to fold the 5"x7" finished frame. She matted the folded frame on 2³/₄"x3³/₄" blue and black rectangles then on black with blue dot and blue solid. The large journaling blocks balance the center photo while the 1³/₄" black and patterned paper squares add embellishment. A page to tickle you pink!

- **patterned Paper Pizazz™:** black/pink/blue stripe, pink tri-dot, black with blue dot (*Bold & Bright*)
- **solid Paper Pizazz™:** black, blue (*Solid Jewel Tones*)
- **2¹/₄" scallop edge punch:** Marvy® Uchida
- **designer:** Arlene Peterson

Susan shows a variation of the folded frame in this page. Following the clothing color, she created a subtle tone-on-tone background by trimming a dark green floral & vines paper to 8"x10¹/₂" and matting it on dark green. She then cut four 3¹/₄"x4¹/₂" rectangles from the light green floral & vines paper, matted them on ivory and placed them evenly spaced on the background. She matted the photo on dark green and positioned it in the center of an 8" square of vellum turned on point. She folded the vellum sides in to meet the photo, then folded the triangle overlap back to meet the edge of the folded frame and finally folded the points in toward the photo. The green matted journaling block and ivory bow finish this tender memory.

- **patterned Paper Pizazz™:** dark green floral & vines, light green floral & vines (*Muted Tints*)
- **specialty Paper Pizazz™:** green vellum (*Pastel Vellum Papers*)
- **solid Paper Pizazz™:** dark green (*Solid Muted Colors*); ivory (*Plain Pastels*)
- **oval die-cut:** Ellison® Craft & Design
- **9" of ⁵/₈" wide ivory sheer ribbon:** C.M. Offray & Son, Inc.
- **green pen:** Zig® Writer
- **designer:** Susan Cobb

Jackets are the perfect place for photos and journaling tags. It's a great technique for adding a different something to your page and they're extra special when made from vellum—who can't resist peeking in a vellum pocket? This is a great technique to use on photo pages when there is a question of who is the subject or a location. Directions for photo and journaling blocks are in the album page descriptions.

This is a beautiful example of a photo pocket page. Susan set the stage with a teal vines patterned paper capturing the background colors and outdoor theme of the photo. She trimmed it to 7¹/₂" wide and cut a rectangle opening before placing it on a coordinating teal stripe background paper. She cut a 5¹/₂"x11" piece of teal vellum and folded the long edges in ¹/₄". Using the triangle pattern, Susan cut a piece out of the top of the vellum and then folded it half to form the pocket. She glued a 5" wide piece of laser lace to the bottom before gluing the pocket over a 2¹/₂" wide vellum strip. The photo was matted on dark teal and silver. Silver pen work and the laser lace glued to the photo mat complete the page. So romantic, Susan!

- **patterned Paper Pizazz™:** teal stripes, teal vines (*Muted Tints*)
- **specialty Paper Pizazz™:** teal vellum (*Pastel Vellum Papers*); specialty silver (by the sheet); laser lace (*Romantic Papers*, also by the sheet)
- **solid Paper Pizazz™:** dark teal (*Solid Jewel Tones*)
- **silver pen:** Sakura Gelly Roll
- **designer:** Susan Cobb

Hailey's all decked out in pink and so's her page. Grandma Arlene not only chronicled Hailey's first Valentine day, she's made a special Valentine for Hailey to discover in the future and tucked it inside a journal pocket. The journal jacket is 3³/₈"x7" pink vellum folded in half with ¹/₈" wide holes punched every ¹/₄" on each side of the pocket. Pink satin ribbon is laced through, glued to the back and two satin bows glued in each corner. A ³/₄" circle punch is used to punch the half-circle at the top. A tiny card made from 3¹/₂"x5" white paper, topped with gingham paper matching the journaling block, a 1¹/₄" wide heart matted on white and trimmed with pattern-edged scissors contains Grandma's message of love for Hailey to discover when she is older. Memories now… memories to come.

- **patterned Paper Pizazz™:** pink flower, pink gingham (*Soft Tints*)
- **specialty Paper Pizazz™:** pink vellum (*Pastel Vellum Papers*)
- **solid Paper Pizazz™:** white (*Plain Pastels*)
- **1¹/₄" wide heart punch:** McGill, Inc.
- **¹/₈" wide hole punch:** Fiskars®, Inc.
- **³/₄" wide hole punch:** Family Treasures, Inc.
- **corkscrew scissors:** Fiskars®, Inc.
- **16" of ¹/₈" wide pink satin ribbon:** C. M. Offray & Son, Inc.
- **white pen:** Pentel Milky Gel Roller
- **designer:** Arlene Peterson

This lavender memory page began when Arlene matted the photo on lavender, lavender/blue floral and lavender again. She cut a 4³/₄"x9¹/₄" strip of blue vellum, trimmed both ends with pattern-edged scissors and centered the photo over it. Lavender pen work and flowers cut from the leftover paper gives it a vintage look. Two 1¹/₂" strips of blue vellum were placed on each side of the photo. 1¹/₄" wide strips of lavender and blue floral paper were trimmed with pattern-edged scissors and glued on the vellum. She cut the journaling jacket 2¹/₂"x6" and folded it in half. The edges were trimmed with pattern-edged scissors and embellished with lavender pen work then glued. She punched a ¹/₂" circle centered on the open edge. The journaling was done on a tag cut from lavender with a ribbon attached through a punched hole. A tender container for a personal remembrance.

- **patterned Paper Pizazz™:** lavender strip, lavender and blue flowers (*Mixing Soft Patterned Papers*)
- **specialty Paper Pizazz™:** blue vellum (*12"x12" Pastel Vellum Papers*, also by the sheet)
- **solid Paper Pizazz™:** lavender (*Plain Pastels*)
- **¹/₈" hole and ¹/₂" circle punches:** Marvy® Uchida
- **gift tag #3 die-cuts:** Accu/Cut® Systems
- **jumbo lace scallop scissors:** Family Treasures, Inc.
- **4" of ¹/₈" wide blue satin ribbon:** C.M. Offray & Son, Inc.
- **lavender pen:** Pentel Hybrid Gel Roller
- **designer:** Arlene Peterson

Those great "before the event" photos are the perfect pages for a journaling jacket. Here everyone's dressed up and looking great. The journal plaque gives the basic information on what and when, but it's the journal pocket that really holds the story. Susan chose a background paper to fit the occasion, trimmed ¹/₂" off each side and matted it on gold paper. She triple matted the photos using colors from the clothing with a complementary accent. She added the journal plaque and then created a journal jacket from metallic vellum. She journaled on the extra vellum from the jacket, punched a hole in the top and tied a ribbon to pull out the sheet. A scatter of snowflakes cut from the vellum scraps and this page is as special as the occasion!

- **patterned Paper Pizazz™:** 12"x12" pine boughs (*Christmas Time*)
- **specialty Paper Pizazz™:** snowflake vellum (*Metallic on Vellum*); metallic gold, metallic silver (*Heavy Metal Papers*)
- **solid Paper Pizazz™:** burgundy, dark blue (*Solid Jewel Tones*)
- **¹/₈" circle punches:** Fiskars®, Inc.
- **oval die-cut:** Ellison Craft® & Design
- **10" of ¹/₄" wide burgundy satin:** C. M. Offray & Son, Inc.
- **gold pen:** Pentel Hybrid Gel Roller
- **designer:** Susan Cobb

Lattice is a lovely technique to give a elegant, airy effect to a page. Lattice can stand on its own as an embellishment or serve as a backdrop for other embellishments. Any paper can be used to create lattice. Patterned papers have white on the reverse side. This will show when folding the lattice strips. It can add a second color to your lattice or two sheets can be glued back to back so the folded portion of the lattice will match the unfolded strips. To make lattice:

On the back of your paper, measure 1³/₄" from the corner on the side to be latticed. Draw a line along the paper then measure 1" down from this mark and mark the paper. Line up a ruler with the second mark and the corner to draw your first angled line. Repeat drawing lines ¹/₂" apart as shown. Cut along the lines.

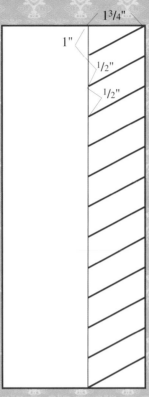

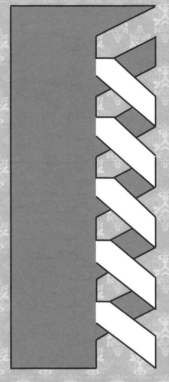

Turn the sheet over and do all the folding next. Fold every other strip. Fold the first strip on top of the strip below it keeping the free edge even with the paper. Skip the next strip. Repeat, folding the third strip as the first. Fold every other strip. Glue the strips together and glue the lattice to the page.

A vellum lattice with a trail of blossoms are all the embellishment needed for this heritage photo. Arlene set the stage by choosing an old-fashion floral to combine with the stripe. She matted the photo on black and then on a rectangle mat of fern vellum over black. Cutting a 6"x8" rectangle of fern vellum, she cut 1³/₄" long angled strips for the lattice before gluing it to the background. She folded and glued the lattice and then the matted photo. The row of flowers were cut from the background paper and glued over the lattice echoing the flowers in the photo. The photo was finished with silver photo corners and two flowers from the background paper. A beautifully preserved past.

- **patterned Paper Pizazz**™: purple flower, purple and green stripe (*Mixing Jewel Patterned Papers*)
- **specialty Paper Pizazz**™: fern vellum (*Vellum Papers*, also by the sheet)
- **solid Paper Pizazz**™: black (*Solid Jewel Tones*)
- **silver photo corners:** Canson-Talens, Inc.
- **silver pen:** Pentel Gel Roller
- **designer:** Arlene Peterson

Mr. & Mrs. Badman 1929

May you always see each other through hearts filled with love.

Vellum papers make this page as soft as a grandma's heart. The photo is matted on white and pink vellum. It is then placed on the pink lattice vellum. The diamonds between the lattice were cut, folded and glued. The lattice was then placed on white dot vellum before being positioned on the pink sponged/floral background. The white vellum repeats the dot in the background paper and helps the diamond cuts stand out. A heart-hugging page.

Grandma BJ & me 2000

Sometimes it's fun just to hang out with my Grandma BJ. She's so funny, she always makes me laugh. We go to movies together and sometimes we bake cookies. I love my Grandma BJ.

- **patterned Paper Pizazz**™: pink sponged/ floral border (*Bj's Handpainted Papers*)
- **specialty Paper Pizazz**™: vellum dots (*Vellum Papers, also by the sheet*); pink lattice vellum (*Soft Patterns in Vellum*); dark pink vellum (*Pastel Vellum Papers*)
- **solid Paper Pizazz**™: white (*Plain Pastels*)
- **X-acto® knife, cutting surface:** Hunt Mfg.
- **designer:** Susan Cobb

Our Little Angel
~2000 Katie 2yrs~

Using tone on tone pattern papers gives a vintage look to this page. Susan matted the "heritage" style photo on white, green vellum and then the green diamond. She cut three diamonds through the vellum on each side, folding and gluing them before matting the photo on the green stripe and finally the green chevron background. The diamond folds add visual interest without "busyness" on this page. A simple touch for a simply adorable page.

- **patterned Paper Pizazz**™: green diamonds, green stripe, green chevron (*Soft Tints*)
- **specialty Paper Pizazz**™: green vellum (*Pastel Vellum Papers*)
- **solid Paper Pizazz**™: white (*Plain Pastels*)
- **X-acto® knife, cutting surface:** Hunt Mfg.
- **black pen:** Zig® Writer
- **designer:** Susan Cobb

Nested motifs are an elegant addition to any page. Although appearing complex, they are easy to create and fit in beautifully as an embellishment or border. To create nested motifs, use our Nested Shapes Template or, trace each piece onto tracing paper. Cut it out and use it as a pattern for vellum, patterned or solid papers. Nested shapes may be finished with pen work or with matting. Arrange them in order of size beginning with the largest piece. Using foam tape between the layers will provide depth or mats may be glued together before being glued to the page. Patterns for the nested shapes used are on the pages with the descriptions given from the bottom layer to the top layer.

For Brynn's page

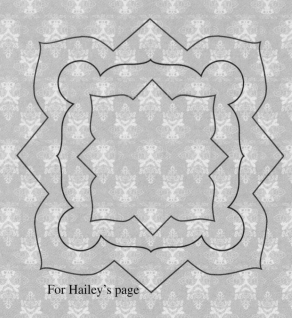

For Hailey's page

This quick-to-make page is lifted to elegance with the addition of the nested motif. Susan cut a sheet of mauve swirl in half on the diagonal and glued it to the striped background. She matted the photos on solid burgundy and attached them with silver photos corners. The nested motif is plum pink vellum, mauve flowers & vines matted on burgundy, mauve swirls matted on burgundy, plum pink vellum and burgundy. All edges were outlined and the flourish in the center of the top burgundy layer was made with a silver pen. A burst of beauty on this tender page.

- **patterned Paper Pizazz™:** mauve swirls, mauve stripe, mauve flowers & vines (*Muted Tints*)
- **specialty Paper Pizazz™:** plum pink vellum (*Pastel Vellum Papers*)
- **solid Paper Pizazz™:** burgundy (*Solid Jewel Tones*)
- **nested template:** *Paper Flair™ Nested Shapes*
- **silver photo corners:** Canson-Talens, Inc.
- **silver pen:** Sakura Gelly Roll
- **designer:** Susan Cobb

Nested motifs in soft patterned colors form a garden of "flowers" on this springtime page. Arlene matted a 4"x12" tan floral strip on cream paper and placed it across the top of the floral stripe background paper. She matted a 1½"x12" tan flower paper on cream and centered it on the floral strip. The center "flower" was created using a tan plaid matted on black, tan flower matted on cream, and tan floral matted on black. The side "flowers" are tan flower matted on black, tan floral matted on cream and tan plaid matted on black. After arranging the nested "flowers" across the tan flower strip, Arlene matted the photos on cream, green, tan plaid and cream again then staggered them on the lower part of the page. A beautiful page with the glow of sunshine.

- **patterned Paper Pizazz™**: floral stripe, tan floral, tan flower, tan plaid (*Mixing Soft Patterned Papers*)
- **solid Paper Pizazz™**: cream (*Plain Pastels*); green (*Solid Jewel Tones*)
- **nested template**: *Paper Flair™ Nested Shapes*
- **foam mounting tape**: Scotch® Brand
- **designer**: Arlene Peterson

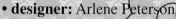

For Missy's page

Arlene created nested motifs to match Hailey's shirt and the medallion on her crown. She matted the photos together on white, blue tri-dot, purple chevron and white again before positioning the photos on the left of the page. She cut a 1¾"x12" strip of the blue tri-dot paper and matted it on white, centering it on the right of the page. A ½"x12" strip of purple gingham was matted on white and centered on the blue strip. Motifs were built from purple chevron, blue tri-dot and purple gingham, each matted on white before being stacked and glued. Placed on both sides of the journaling block, this page moves from simple to simply marvelous.

- **patterned Paper Pizazz™**: lavender swirl, lavender gingham (*Soft Tints,* also by the sheet); lavender chevrons, blue tri-dot (*Soft Tints*)
- **solid Paper Pizazz™**: white (*Plain Pastels*)
- **nested template**: *Paper Flair™ Nested Shapes*
- **designer**: Arlene Peterson

What a fun way to design and build a page! Squares, blocks and triangles offer an infinite number of ways to put together marvelous looking pages and use up scraps, too! Lay out your design and play with it until it's what you want before you glue the pieces into place. To get uniform sizes and shapes, make templates out of cardstock to use when cutting your papers.

Incorporating vellum into triangles gives your pages the light look. Arlene matted the photo on vellum and centered it on the peach floral background paper. Using a simple square cut on the diagonal to form triangles, she constructed the marvelous border. She cut four 3" peach vellum squares for the corners and twelve 1³/4" squares cut diagonally for the triangles. She cut four 2³/4" peach check squares and six 1¹/2" squares. Each was cut on the diagonal with the larger triangles glued over the corner vellum squares and the smaller triangles glued over the peach vellum triangles. So simple…so satisfying.

- **patterned Paper Pizazz™:** 12"x12" peach check, (*Soft Florals & Patterns*); peach roses (*Soft Florals & Patterns,* also by the sheet)
- **specialty Paper Pizazz™:** peach vellum (*Pastel Vellum Papers*)
- **designer:** Arlene Peterson

This page is pillow soft and baby sweet with its blend of lavender patterns and laser lace. Beginning with a pale yellow background paper, Susan used four lavender stripe and four laser lace diamonds to create the center diamond. She then inset 1⁷/8" lace and floral squares alternating with stripe and floral diamonds in the points of the center star. The spaces between were filled with floral triangles and bordered with the lavender lattice. The photos were matted on pale yellow and then white. Their placement in the corners is a natural extension of the page's design. A purple satin ribbon ties this page up neatly.

- **patterned Paper Pizazz™:** lavender stripe, lavender lattice (*Soft Florals & Patterns*); lavender roses (*Soft Florals & Patterns,* also by the sheet)
- **specialty Paper Pizazz™:** laser lace (*Romantic Papers,* also by the sheet)
- **solid Paper Pizazz™:** white, pale yellow (*Solid Pastel Papers*)
- **12" of ⁵/8" wide lavender satin ribbon:** C.M. Offray & Son, Inc.
- **silver pen:** Sakura Gelly Roll
- **designer:** Susan Cobb

Once the photos were "squared" away, triangles became the basic building block of this page. The photos were matted on tan and placed in opposite corners of a 9" square. Same size rectangles balanced out the space. The green triangles in the borders form a pattern called "flying geese" and are $1^1/2$" squares cut on the diagonal. The burgundy triangles are cut from 1" squares. Triangles can overlap to form a kaleidoscope effect like in the corner square. The dark, warm colors are a wonderful choice for this page, matching the clothing and the season.

- **patterned Paper Pizazz™**: forest green suede (by the sheet); burgundy and tan leaf, burgundy/purple geometric (*Mixing Jewel Patterned Papers*)
- **solid Paper Pizazz™**: tan (*Solid Pastel Papers*)
- **designer**: Arlene Peterson

Blocks, squares and triangles are a marvelous technique for mixing patterns on your page. Arlene shows us how! Although she uses five patterns, she uses only two colors. Pink and yellow gingham is the background because it matched Hailey's dress and toy while the matting paper matches her collar and shoes. The swirl and squiggle work well together. The flowers and dots echo and balance. The piecing was consistent. All the triangles are floral and dot and cut from $1^1/2$" squares. All the $^7/8$"x$1^3/4$" rectangles are swirl and squiggle. If you look closely at the corner squares you'll see they are made up of tiny blocks identically put together like the big blocks. Nice "piece" of work, Arlene!

- **patterned Paper Pizazz™**: pink swirl, pink/yellow gingham, pink flower, yellow dot, yellow squiggle (*Soft Tints*)
- **solid Paper Pizazz™**: white (*Plain Pastels*)
- **black pen**: Sakura Gelly Roll
- **designer**: Arlene Peterson

If you've ever wished you had more room on your page for additional photos or journaling, these interactive pages will show you how to find the room you want. Folding cards, mini albums and accordion style booklets are marvelous page stretchers!

Clever use of a blank card turns this 8¹/₂"x11" page into a whole storybook! Susan trimmed 1" from the top and right side of the vellum snowflakes paper and glue it centered on the blue stripe paper. She trimmed a 5"x6¹/₂" blank card to 5" square. She glued blue snowflake paper to the card front. She cut a 5"x10" piece of blue vellum snowflake paper and glued the bottom half to the inside card front aligning the edges. She cut a 5"x10" sheet of the blue snowflake paper and glued the top half to the inside back of the card, aligning the edges. Fill with photos, journaling and embellishments. Fold the sheets in half and glue light blue to the back of the snowflakes. Close the card for your storybook. Glue the back of the card to the page. There will be wonderful memories to be told within these pages!

Open

Open

Open

- **patterned Paper Pizazz™:** 2 sheets of blue snowflakes (*Christmas*, also by the sheet); blue stripe (*Bright Tints*)
- **specialty Paper Pizazz™:** vellum blue snowflakes (by the sheet); vellum snowflakes (*Vellum Papers*, also by the sheet)
- **solid Paper Pizazz™:** light blue, white (*Plain Pastels*)
- **5"x6¹/₂" white blank card:** Paper Flair™
- **snowflake #3 die-cut:** Accu/Cut® Systems
- **³/₈", ¹/₂", 1" snowflake punches:** Marvy® Uchida
- **white pen:** Pentel Milky Gel Roller
- **blue pen:** Zig® Writer
- **designer:** Susan Cobb

A wonderful way to tell a story is through photo journaling! Susan began by cutting two pieces of 8"x6" white paper and folding them in half to form the booklet. She placed a green vellum matted photo and journaling on each page then tied it together with ribbon. She cut a sheet of rose leaves paper to 8¹/₂"x8". A 2³/₄" square window was cut in the paper. A 1¹/₄"x7" rose stripe was cut and centered above and below the window. Extra stripes formed a frame around the window. The rose leaves paper was glued to form a flap over the top of the rose flourishes background paper and a 8¹/₂"x5" piece of coral vellum formed a flap over the lower section of the background paper. The photo journal was centered under the window in the top flap and the journaling block under the vellum flap. A page rich with memories!

oval ©&™ Ellison® Craft & Design

- **patterned Paper Pizazz™:** rose leaves, rose flourishes, rose stripes (*Muted Tints*)
- **specialty Paper Pizazz™:** sage vellum, coral vellum (*Pastel Vellum Papers*)
- **solid Paper Pizazz™:** white (*Plain Pastels*)
- **oval die-cut:** Ellison® Craft & Design
- **28" of ¹/₄" wide white satin ribbon:** C.M. Offray & Son, Inc.
- **silver pen:** Sakura Gelly Roll
- **designer:** Susan Cobb

Photos on next page.

Kaelin's first birthday is not only wrapped in this delightful page but the gift tag holds more photos and journaling. Susan cut two 2"x12" strips of blue posies paper, matted them on white trimmed with patterned-edged scissors then glued them on a 12"x12" sheet of blue gingham. The corners of the gingham and the edges of the posies paper were chalked. A 2"x7" strip was transformed into the bow and a 2"x5" strip became the center loop. Susan folded a 5$^1/_8$"x12" piece of the blue posies paper and folded it every 3$^3/_8$" into an accordion. She then cut a 5$^1/_8$"x6$^3/_4$" strip of blue striped paper and folded it into an accordion. She glued one section from each piece together forming a long accordion then refolded the papers before using the template to cut out the gift tag shape. She matted the first section with white trimmed with patterned-edged scissors, then blue vellum and punched the hole. After filling the book with photos and journaling, she tied it with a satin bow, gluing the ends under the paper bow. A sweet treat of a page!

- **patterned Paper Pizazz™**: blue gingham, blue posies, blue stripes (*12"x12" Soft Tints,* also by the sheet)
- **specialty Paper Pizazz™**: blue vellum (*12"x12" Pastel Vellum Papers,* also by the sheet)
- **solid Paper Pizazz™**: white (*Solid Pastel Papers*)
- **¼" wide circle punch**: McGill, Inc.

- **mini scallop scissors**: Fiskars®, Inc.
- **blue decorative chalk**: Craf-T Products
- **24" of ¼" wide white satin ribbon**: C.M. Offray & Son, Inc.
- **black pen**: Zig® Millenium
- **designer**: Susan Cobb

Bargello was originally a needlework technique using long stitches to create beautiful designs. Through the centuries, bargello has adapted to many forms and now it appears in its beautiful diversity on scrapbook pages. Strips of mixed and matched papers create the bargello effect. To make bargello:

Select your papers and cut strips 1/4"–3/4" wide. A designer tip is to take two sheets of white paper and lay it over patterned papers in different directions and widths to see cutting options.

Arrange the strips on a mat. When satisfied with your design, glue into place. Leaving space between strips is another design option. Use additional strips to border your design. If you are placing bargello over patterned papers, follow the "Golden Rule" and leave a border of plain matting.

Bargello creates a lovely block adding visual interest to this page. Susan began with an 8" square of white paper. She cut 5/8" wide strips of lavender lattice paper and 7/16" wide strips of lavender stripe paper. Leaving a 1/16" space around the edges and between the strips, she bordered opposite sides of the square with the strips. She then placed perpendicular strips between the end borders with 1" laser lace squares postioned in the corners. The remaining strips were used to fill the center. The photos and journal block were matted with lavender vellum. The bargello block was centered on point over the floral paper background with the journal block echoing the position. A lovely way to use up scraps!

- **patterned Paper Pizazz**™: lavender stripe, lavender lattice (*Soft Florals & Patterns*), lavender roses (*Soft Florals & Patterns*, also by the sheet)
- **specialty Paper Pizazz**™: lavender vellum (*Pastel Vellum Papers*); laser lace (*Romantic Papers*, also by the sheet)
- **solid Paper Pizazz**™: white (*Plain Pastels*)
- **silver pen:** Sakura Gelly Roll
- **designer:** Susan Cobb

If you would love to create a bargello background but wonder if it would be too busy, Arlene shows how to keep your photos the focus of the page. Using three patterns, she cut 3/8" wide strips of the multi-color reflections paper, 1/2" wide strips of the orange tile paper, and 3/4" wide strips of the blue ripple paper. She placed 7 1/2" long strips on a 12"x12" black paper beginning at the upper left corner and ending at the lower right. A narrow strip of black shows between each strip. She covered the ends of the strips with an orange tiles strip and then worked the pattern out to the remaining corners. She matted two photos as one on black, multi-color reflections and black. This gives the photos more impact than being individually matted. By placing the photos square on the page, they stand out against the bargello background. Awesome page, Arlene!

- **patterned Paper Pizazz™:** multi-color reflections, orange tiles, blue ripple (*Great Backgrounds*)
- **solid Paper Pizazz™:** black (*Solid Jewel Tones*); 12"x12" black (*Coordinating Colors™ Black & White*)
- **designer:** Arlene Peterson

Bargello not only works behind the "scenes", it is great in a leading role. Arlene chose a green flourish background paper then matted the photo five times on green, black and stripe. Check out how she cut strips of the stripe and positioned them around the matted photo so they form a frame. She created bargello corners using 3/4" wide purple flower paper, 1/2" wide stripe and 3/8" wide purple sprig paper, place on a black mat and, leaving a 1/16" black border on the long edge. The corners were placed, overlapping slightly and giving the effect of a "lens" opening on this heritage scene. A glance to the past done beautifully.

- **patterned Paper Pizazz™:** green flourish, purple/green stripe, purple sprig, purple flower (*Mixing Soft Patterned Papers*)
- **solid Paper Pizazz™:** black, green (*Solid Jewel Tones*); cream (*Plain Pastels*)
- **designer:** Arlene Peterson

Vellum bouquet holders bring a breath of beauty to an album page. Filled with beautiful flowers cut from floral vellum papers and tied with bows, they add a sweet touch that will never wilt. To make a vellum bouquet holder:

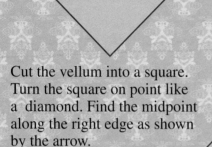
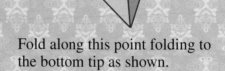

Cut the vellum into a square. Turn the square on point like a diamond. Find the midpoint along the right edge as shown by the arrow.

Fold along this point folding to the bottom tip as shown.

Find the midpoint along the left edge and fold.

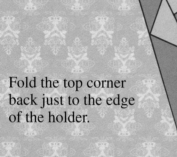

Fold the top corner back just to the edge of the holder.

Fold the next layer back to the edge of the holder.

Vellum bouquet holders can come in any size. Here Susan used a 5" square of vellum to create the holder for this page. Filled with vellum roses and ferns, the vellum bouquet holder is a major element. The mauve and dark blue matted photo and journal block were placed on a floral clusters vellum sheet over the pink satin background. The bouquet balances the photo and illustrates the type of tribute a young woman might receive at her graduation. A wonderfully feminine page.

- **patterned Paper Pizazz™:** pink satin (*Very Pretty Papers*)
- **specialty Paper Pizazz™:** vellum florals and ferns, floral cluster and dots (*Heritage Vellum*)
- **oval die-cut:** Ellison® Craft & Design
- **solid Paper Pizazz™:** mauve (*Solid Muted Colors*); dark blue (*Solid Jewel Tones*)
- **gold photo corners:** Canson-Talens, Inc.
- **9" of 3/8" wide dusty pink satin ribbon:** C.M. Offray & Son, Inc.
- **gold pen:** Pentel Hybrid Gel Roller
- **designer:** Susan Cobb

oval ©&™ Ellison® Craft & Design

This page and the vellum bouquet holder spill over with summer as Susan catches the feel and colors of a June afternoon. An overall patterned floral vellum covers the corners of the yellow squiggle paper. Strips of 1/8" wide white paper are glued over the edges. Flowers and butterflies were cut from the matching floral vellum border paper and now trail out of a small bouquet holder made from a 3" square of blue vellum. The photo is matted on blue vellum and white for a beautiful, barefoot kind of page.

- **patterned Paper Pizazz™:** blue gingham, yellow squiggle (*Soft Tints*)
- **specialty Paper Pizazz™:** vellum floral clusters, vellum field of flowers (*Floral Vellum Papers*); baby blue vellum (*Pastel Vellum Papers*)
- **solid Paper Pizazz™:** white (*Plain Pastels*)
- **9" of 1/8" wide blue satin ribbon:** C.M. Offray & Son, Inc.
- **baby blue pen:** Zig® Writer
- **designer:** Susan Cobb

Just like love and marriage, bouquets and brides go together. Beginning with a 12"x12" sponged background paper, Susan layered a sheet of roses vellum edged with silver pen on the left side of the background. She matted the photo on pale yellow and lavender vellum. She punched out the corners and wound silver thread around it finishing in a bow. She added blue vellum and vellum net mats before positioning it over the roses vellum paper. Susan used a 3 1/2" square of vellum net to make the bouquet holder; filled it with flowers cut from a second roses vellum sheet and tied it with metallic silver thread. A once in a lifetime beautiful page.

- **patterned Paper Pizazz™:** purple sponged (*Very Pretty Papers*)
- **specialty Paper Pizazz™:** vellum netting (*Lacy Vellum*); roses vellum (*Floral Vellum Papers*); lavender vellum, blue vellum (*Pastel Vellum Papers*)
- **solid Paper Pizazz™:** pale yellow (*Plain Pastels*)
- **notch corner punch:** Marvy® Uchida
- **metallic silver thread:** Westrim® Crafts
- **silver pen:** Sakura Gelly Roll
- **designer:** Susan Cobb

Collage is the perfect reason to save every leftover bit of your scrapbooking papers. A rich story can be built up as papers are layered and embellishments added to create a treasured memory.

Shauna used collage to capture Earle's world-wide career as a conductor. She layered torn-edged music paper on the background paper. She tucked postcards torn from patterned paper under the edge of the music paper and a piece of lace paper under the photo matted on gold and torn black papers. The metallic music note vellum border was torn, layered over the edge of the photo and held in place with gold brads. A treble clef charm was tied with gold thread to a gold-edged sheer ribbon before being glued in the corner of the photo. Foam tape mounted "stamps" (cut from patterned paper), clock charms and a strand of beads finish this symphony of memories.

- **patterned Paper Pizazz™:** postcards, stamps (*Heritage Papers*, also by the sheet); letters, antique lace (*Black & White Photos*, also by the sheet); sheet music (*Vintage Papers*), gold with black border (by the sheet)
- **specialty Paper Pizazz™:** gold music on vellum (*Metallic on Vellum*); gold (*Metallic Papers*)
- **solid Paper Pizazz™:** black (*Solid Jewel Tones*)
- **treble clef, clock charms:** Creative Beginnings
- **6" of metallic gold thread:** Coats & Clark
- **12" of fused gold beads:** Wrights®
- **5" of gold-edged sheer ribbon:** C.M. Offray & Son, Inc.
- **gold brads:** AmericanPin/HyGlo
- **foam mounting tape:** Scotch® Brand
- **black pen:** Sakura Gelly Roll
- **designer:** Shauna Berglund-Immel

Shauna carried the pride of her country into this page. She chose three different patterned papers to create the background. She layered 1"x12" torn strips of red floral over the white lace background paper and then topped it with a 4"x12" torn-edge blue fleur-de-lis paper. The photos were matted on gold and the blue fleur-de-lis paper topped with gold-edged sheer ribbons. Die-cut letters edged with gold pen, gold journaling, and paper embellishments complete this family's salute to their country.

- **patterned Paper Pizazz™:** white lace (*Our Wedding Day*); red floral, blue fleur-de-lis (*Collage Papers*); stars, eagle (*Embellishments*)
- **specialty Paper Pizazz™:** specialty gold (*Metallic Papers*, also by the sheet)
- **1¼" traveler letter die-cuts:** Accu/Cut® Systems
- **8" of ⅝" wide gold-edged sheer ribbon:** C.M. Offray & Son, Inc.
- **black pen:** Sakura Gelly Roll
- **gold pen:** Pentel Hybrid Gel Roller
- **designer:** Shauna Berglund-Immel

LeNae had a rippin' good time creating the backgrounds for these pages. She chose three complementary patterns in purples to match the background in the photo. She then tore each sheet into three pieces and created two new sheets by gluing one piece of each together to form an 8¹/2"x11" page. She used identical matting on the photos for both pages— white trimmed with pattern-edged scissors, purple dot with an offset mat of purple vellum. She tilted the photos in opposite directions for visual interest. The journaling letters were cut from the remaining pieces of the paper using a template. LeNae says to get the white edge on the torn papers, pull up on the paper as you tear.

- **patterned Paper Pizazz™:** purple moiré, purple sponged, hydrangeas (*Pretty Papers,* also by the sheets); purple dots (*Soft Tints*)
- **specialty Paper Pizazz™:** purple vellum (*Pastel Vellum Papers*)
- **solid Paper Pizazz™:** white (*Plain Pastels*)
- **mini antique Victorian scissors:** Family Treasures, Inc.
- **alphabet template:** Frances Meyer, Inc.® Fat Caps
- **black pen:** Sakura Gelly Roll
- **designer:** LeNae Gerig

Susan says it's marvelously easy to create a collage page when you use a coordinating family of paper. She layered a 4¹/2"x12" strip of black with vines 1" from the left on the small floral patterned background paper. A 9" square of the large floral was matted on tan and glued centered on the page. A piece of 7¹/4"x8¹/4" tan vellum was centered on the right side and a 4⁵/8"x7¹/2" piece of black with vines glued on it. She matted a 2¹/8"x12" strip of the large floral on black and glued it across the middle of the page. The photo was matted on ivory, tan vellum and tan solid paper. It was held with black photo corners and the page finished with a black matted tan journal plaque and a sheer beige bow. Timeless appeal.

- **patterned Paper Pizazz™:** black with vines, small floral, large floral (*Mixing Heritage Papers*)
- **specialty Paper Pizazz™:** tan vellum (*12"x12" Pastel Vellum Papers,* also by the sheet)
- **solid Paper Pizazz™:** tan, ivory (*Solid Pastel Papers*); black (*Solid Jewel Tones*)
- **oval template:** ESP Crafts
- **black photo corners:** Canson-Talens, Inc.
- **9" of ⁵/8" wide sheer beige ribbon:** C.M. Offray & Son, Inc.
- **black pen:** Zig® Writer
- **designer:** Susan Cobb

Paper can be tied in a knot, turned into bows or laced just like ribbon. When using patterned papers, cut double the strips you'll need. Glue two strips back to back so the white side is covered. This isn't necessary for vellum. Paper must be handled gently as you form a knot or bow. Don't tug—instead pull or push lightly with your fingers as you tighten the knot. Using longer strips allows for easier tying. It's "knot" hard to add some fun touches to your pages.

After doing some knifework around the beach pebbles, LeNae slipped in a sheet of green vellum and placed the black matted photos. Then she caught a great idea when she decided to finish this page with "burlap" knots. She cut two 1¼"x11" strips of burlap paper. She drew black pen "stitches" along the edges before knotting them. Since these embellishments were to be glued down, she tied the knot and then carefully twisted the paper so the white side was glued to the background. A rock-solid technique, LeNae!

- **patterned Paper Pizazz™:** 12"x12" beach pebbles (by the sheet); burlap (*Country*, also by the sheet)
- **specialty Paper Pizazz™:** green vellum (*Pastel Vellum Papers*)
- **solid Paper Pizazz™:** black (*Solid Jewel Tones*)
- **X-acto® knife, cutting surface:** Hunt Mfg.
- **black pen:** Zig® Writer
- **designer:** LeNae Gerig

Amy rounds this page up and ties it down right nice. She begins with a denim background and then trims 1½" off a long and short side of the country dot paper and centers it on the background paper. Using twelve ³/₁₆"x11" strips of paper, she glues them back-to-back to form six strips. She cuts ¼" long parallel slits in the dot and denim papers 1" apart. The strips are fed down one hole and up through the adjacent hole, knotted and tails trimmed to ³/₈" long. The photos and journal blocks were matted on white and then brown suede. Position the photos after you've completed the paper knots. Yippee-*tie*-yo, pardner!

- **patterned Paper Pizazz™:** brown suede (*Making Heritage*, also by the sheet); country dots, denim (*Country*, also by the sheet)
- **solid Paper Pizazz™:** white (*Plain Pastels*)
- **designer:** Amy Gustafson

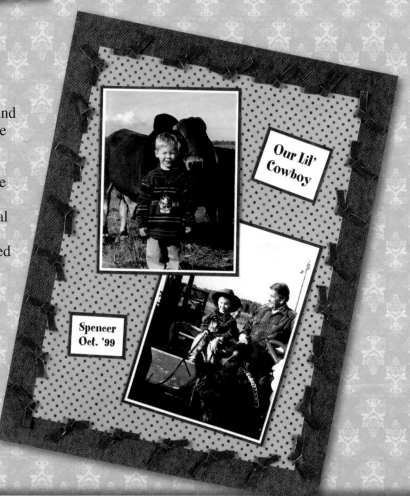

Not only can you tie a page down with knots, you can lace it right up, too! Susan matted Janae's photo on white and then positioned it on the right side of the pink screen mat. She punched nine sets of holes along the left side. She then cut six 11" strips from the pink dot paper to the width of one large dot and glued them back to back. Beginning at the top, she laced one strip down through 8 holes (just like lacing your shoes), gluing it to the back of the page at the top and bottom. Then she repeated with the second strip. She used the third strip in the bottom two holes and tied a knot. Susan recommends using a rectangle punch for lacing holes. A dandy effect…a darling page.

- **patterned Paper Pizazz™**: pink screen, pink lattice, pink dots (*Bright Tints*)
- **solid Paper Pizazz™**: white (*Plain Pastels*); goldenrod (*Plain Brights*)
- **³⁄₁₆" rectangle, ¹⁄₂" daisy, ¹⁄₈" circle punches**: Fiskars®, Inc.
- **black pen**: Zig® Writer
- **designer**: Susan Cobb

Janae
Our
Little Miss Sunshine
Summer
2001

Bows as soft as a baby's dreams. The gossamer bows on this page were made from vellum! Amy used seven ³⁄₁₆"x11" strips. She cut five strips in half to make the bows. Amy says pull very gently when making vellum bows. The fragile paper will tear easily! After the bottom border was matted on white, ¹⁄₄" slits were cut every ¹⁄₂" across the center. Beginning one at each end, the remaining two strips of vellum were woven through the slits. The ends were trimmed and a bow glued over them at the center. A dreamy page.

- **patterned Paper Pizazz™**: pink with roses, blue with rosebuds, green with white dots (*Mixing Soft Patterned Papers*)
- **specialty Paper Pizazz™**: pink vellum (*Pastel Vellum Papers*)
- **solid Paper Pizazz™**: white (*Solid Pastel Papers*)
- **alphabet template**: Frances Meyer, Inc.®
- **black pen**: Sakura Gelly Roll
- **designer**: Amy Gustafson

My beautiful niece Rachael Janae was born on March 21, 2001, in Hayward, CA. Chris called us when Jenny went into labor and Mom, Dad, Geoff, and I drove through the night to get down there! We met Rachael when she was about 4 hours old. I took this picture of her napping on Grandpa's lap when they came up to visit us in April. Rachael was one month old.

Flowers add beauty and polish to any occasion and they can do the same on your pages. Flowers can be strewn as a borders or arranged as an individual element. Whether they echo the photo or highlight the theme, they are always the perfect touch. To make roses and rosebuds:

Cut five petals for each rose from this pattern. Cut four petals for each rosebud.

Apply glue along the bottom edge of one petal and roll into a cylinder. Pinch the bottom together.

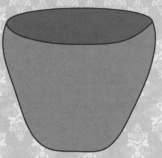

With the other petals, fold the top edge back.

Apply glue to the bottom edge of the petal, then pinch at the bottom.

Wrap the petal around the cylinder.

Pinch and glue the bottom edges together. Repeat with each petal over lapping the previous petal slightly.

Say it with roses and Mike said it magnificently with his anniversary bouquet. LeNae created a lovely tribute page capturing the roses forever in a vellum vase. She matted the photo on black and then on a torn red rose paper. She made four red "roses" and one pink "rosebud" from handmade papers (see directions above). After tracing the vase on vellum with black pen, she cut it out just outside the lines. She cut and glued the 3/16" wide stems and 1¹/4" long leaves from green paper. The vellum vase was glued over the stems and the "roses" to the tops of the stems. The journaling completes this true love page.

- **patterned Paper Pizazz™:** 12"x12" red roses (by the sheet)
- **specialty Paper Pizazz™:** vellum dots (*Vellum Papers*, also by the sheet)
- **solid Paper Pizazz™:** green (*Solid Muted Colors*); black (*Solid Jewel Tones*)
- **red and pink handmade paper:** Black Ink
- **white pen:** Pentel Milky Gel Roller
- **black pen:** Zig® Writer
- **designer:** LeNae Gerig

– A True Romantic –

This year for our wedding Anniversary Mike gave me 37 red roses, one for each year of our marriage. This has become our tradition. He always includes a single pink rose bud to symbolize the year to come. He makes me feel so special. August 2001

Daisies were popping up all over in this photo so LeNae used a whole field of them for this page. She chose the mat colors from the ladybugs happily traveling through the daisy paper. After matting the photos and journal block on white, red and black, she decided a daisy chain would be the perfect border. She cut 2¼" black with white dots squares and matted them on red. She cut a ⅜"x8½" strip of red and glued it 2" from the bottom of the page. The three squares were glued evenly spaced. LeNae drew the daisy petal patterns on the back of white paper and tore out eight petals for each daisy and punched two ½" wide yellow circles for each. She glue the petals on the squares and the corner of the photo. LeNae lightly chalked the center of the petals blue, glued a yellow circle over the middle, then placed a tiny square of foam tape on the circle and placed a second punched circle on top of the foam for dimension. Isn't this a happy page!

- **patterned Paper Pizazz™:** ladybugs (by the sheet); black with white dots (*Coordinating Colors™ Black & White*)
- **solid Paper Pizazz™:** yellow, white (*Plain Pastels*); red (*Plain Brights*); black (*Solid Jewel Tones*)
- **blue decorative chalk:** Craf-T Products
- **½" wide circle punch:** Family Treasures, Inc.
- **foam mounting tape:** Scotch® Brand
- **designer:** LeNae Gerig

The sea of tulips blossoming behind LeNae and Lauren inspired LeNae to plant her own row of flowers. She tore a 3"x8½" strip of green screen paper and glued it 1" from the bottom of the page. She drew petal shapes on the back of the red and yellow papers and tore out four petals for each blossom. She rolled the top edge under and pinched the bottom together before gluing the petals to the border strip. Strips of ½" wide green paper were torn and glued into place for the stems. Torn leaves completed the border. The photo was matted on white and trimmed with pattern-edged scissors. Red and yellow rectangles were torn and glued at an angle over the green diamond background with the photo centered on them. Bloomin' beautiful, LeNae.

- **patterned Paper Pizazz™:** green diamonds, green screen (*Bright Tints*)
- **solid Paper Pizazz™:** yellow, red (*Plain Brights*); dark green (*Solid Jewel Tones*)
- **ripple scissors:** Fiskars®, Inc.
- **black pen:** Zig® Writer
- **designer:** LeNae Gerig

Memories of time spent with friends from Japan were captured in this east/west page. LeNae cut a 2½"x12" strip of blue/green fans, matted it on a 3⅛"x12" strip of ivory "handmade" paper and glued it 1" from the left of the 12"x12" aqua blue "handmade" background paper. She die-cut kanji characters from solid black paper, gluing them evenly spaced over the "ribbon". The photo was matted on black and placed in the upper section of the page. The west was represented with a branch of dogwood. She used black pen to draw the branch. She cut four petals for each blossom from the ivory "handmade" paper. She nipped out the characteristic scallop on the edge with a hole punch and pinched the opposite end together before gluing on the branch. She punched holes of brown paper and glued them to the center of the dogwood blossoms.

To get the Asian style journaling, LeNae suggests printing out the journaling on the computer using an Asian font. Then use a light table or window and trace over it with the brush marker on the background paper. Kanji patterns on page 144.

- **patterned Paper Pizazz™:** blue handmade, ivory handmade (*The "Handmade" Look*); blue/green fans (*Mixing Jewel Patterned Papers*)
- **solid Paper Pizazz™:** black, brown (*Solid Jewel Tones*)
- **¼" hole punch:** McGill, Inc.
- **kanji character die-cuts:** Accu/Cut® Systems
- **black pen:** Zig® Brush Marker
- **designer:** LeNae Gerig

Spring flowers cheerfully clamor up a trellis heralding the Easter season as the family gathers to celebrate. LeNae created the lattice by cutting two ½"x12" strips, gluing the first strip ¾" from the left edge of the 12"x12" background paper and the second 13/16" from the first. She cut eight ½"x3¼" strips and glued them evenly spaced across the long strips. She used brown chalk to shade the lattice. The photos were matted on green and then placed on a 5¼"x11" strip of vellum dot paper. A 7½"x8" rectangle of roses was centered on the background and the vellum mat glued over it.

To create the flowers, LeNae cut four pieces of both vellum and rose paper 1¼"x5" long. She made ⅛"x1" cuts across the strip. Glue was applied across the bottom of the vellum strip and it was rolled up. The rose strip was glued, rolled around the vellum and the edges curled with the straight edge of scissors. A happy spring page.

- **patterned Paper Pizazz™:** roses (by the sheet); 12"x12" forest green suede (by the sheet)
- **specialty Paper Pizazz™:** vellum dots (*Vellum Papers,* by the sheet)
- **solid Paper Pizazz™:** 12"x12" white (*Solid Pastel Papers*); green (*Solid Muted Papers*)
- **brown decorative chalk:** Craf-T products
- **black pen:** Zig® Writer
- **designer:** LeNae Gerig

A little girl dances in the sun and the world dances with her in this charming page. LeNae started with a sunny background paper. She cut $5^1/4$"x$6^3/8$" blue and pink vellum rectangles, angling them on the page. The photo was matted with white and trimmed with pattern-edged scissors. A 2"x$8^1/2$" strip of purple dot paper was matted on white and trimmed with pattern-edged scissors then glued $^1/2$" from the top of the background. Delicate mums were made from vellum, their petal shapes echoing Emily's skirt. LeNae cut 16 petals each from the pink, yellow and blue vellum. She folded the petals, and using a glue dot, placed eight petals in the first layer, she added another glue dot and placed eight more in a second layer. She punched holes from contrasting vellum, gluing them to form the center of the flowers. A lovely swirl of a page!

- **patterned Paper Pizazz**™: yellow stripe, purple dot (*Soft Tints*)
- **specialty Paper Pizazz**™: blue, yellow, pink, purple vellum (*Pastel Vellum Papers*)
- **solid Paper Pizazz**™: white (*Plain Pastels*)
- **$^1/4$" hole punch:** McGill, Inc.
- **seagull and ripple scissors:** Fiskars®, Inc.
- **glue dots:** Glue Dots International LLC
- **black pen:** Zig® Writer
- **designer:** LeNae Gerig

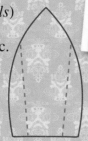

Emily 2001

4 yrs. old

Hawaii 2001

Soft tropical breezes blow and mulberry paper flowers drift across the page. The four flower petals for each blossom were torn from the mulberry paper and lightly chalked. To achieve the feathery edges, moisten the paper before tearing. The buds were torn and folded into a cone shape. The mat was torn from green mulberry paper with leaves torn from the remainder. The flower centers were rolled from 1" square paper scraps into small balls. After matting the photo on blue, the green mat was placed with the photo glued over it. The leaves, flower petals, buds and center were arranged and glued into place. A beauty of a page!

- **patterned Paper Pizazz**™: blue floral (*Collage Papers*)
- **solid Paper Pizazz**™: blue (*Plain Pastels*)
- **green, pink, yellow mulberry papers:** Black Ink
- **yellow, dark green, pink, orange decorative chalks:** Craf-T Products
- **black pen:** Zig® Writer
- **designer:** LeNae Gerig

Okay, it's time to get in shape! We're talking about shaping your pages…literally. Our designers will teach you to bend and stretch your pages into fabulous forms. You are going to love these workouts!

LeNae wraps up Madison's birthday in a great big gift package. She trimmed the pink and yellow gingham to a 2¹/₄"x11³/₄" strip and matted it on white. The yellow with pink flowers was cut to an 11" square and matted on white. A ³/₄"x 12" wide pink strip was matted on white and then glue angled across the lower right corner and trimmed. The rest of the strip was glue to the upper left corner. The bow was cut out of pink matted on white with black pen details and glued to the top of the package. The gift tag was punched and hung with gold thread from the bow. The photos were matted on pink then white and finished with pattern-edged scissors and black pen dots. To be opened anytime for sweet memories. Bow pattern on page 141.

- **patterned Paper Pizazz™:** pink/yellow gingham, yellow/pink posies (*12"x12" Soft Tints,* also by the sheet)
- **solid Paper Pizazz™:** 12"x12" white, pink (*Solid Pastel Papers*)
- **¹/₈" hole punch:** McGill, Inc.
- **foam mounting tape:** Scotch® Brand
- **mini scallop scissors:** Fiskars®, Inc.
- **6" of gold metallic thread:** Westrim®, Inc.
- **black pen:** Zig® Millenium
- **designer:** LeNae Gerig

What a turkey of a page! And what better way to show off your Thanksgiving season pictures. Follow the pattern on page 143 to make the turkey body then mat on black. Cut as many feathers as you need, using a variety of patterned papers, to fit around the body. Mat each on black. Cut and mat the beak, wattle and bow. Draw the eyes and bow detail with black pen. The tail feathers will extend beyond the page protector. LeNae says place the page protector over your completed turkey and mark the edges, then trim the feathers to fit. Add your photos, journaling block and serve with love.

- **patterned Paper Pizazz™:** brown plaid (*Great Outdoors,* also by the sheet); brown stripe, brown with stars, brown check (*Coordinating Colors™ Brown & White*); red velvet (*Textured Papers*); green dots (*Bright Tints*); handmade brown (*The Handmade Look*)
- **solid Paper Pizazz™:** 12"x12" black (*Coordinating Colors™ Black & White*); orange (*Solid Muted Colors*)
- **black pen:** Zig® Writer
- **designer:** LeNae Gerig

Have a ball with your scrapbook page…a Christmas ball. Start by drawing an 11³/₄" circle on the 12"x12" green with white dots paper and the white paper. Trace the "snowy edge" pattern on the top ¹/₃ of the white circle and trim. Trim an additional ¹/₂" from the top of the white. Glue into place, leaving room for the hanger. Trace and cut the white highlights, mat on black and glue in place. Trace the hanger onto the gray paper, cut out, and trim the bottom with pattern-edged scissors. Mat on black and trim again. Use the red with white dot paper for the bow pieces, repeating the tracing, cutting and matting. Using the black pen, add journaling and details to the "snowy top", bow and bulb hanger. Mat the photos on red then black. Trim with pattern-edged scissors and place dots in the scallops using the white pen. Happy Holidays! Patterns on page 142.

- **patterned Paper Pizazz™:** 12"x12" green with white dots, red with white dots (*Christmas Time*, also by the sheet)
- **solid Paper Pizazz™:** 12"x12" black, white (*Coordinating Colors™ Black & White*); red (*Plain Brights*); gray (*Solid Jewel Tones*)
- **ripple and corkscrew scissors:** Fiskars®, Inc.
- **black pen:** Zig® Writer
- **white pen**: Pentel Milky Gel Roller
- **designer:** LeNae Gerig

Tuck your favorite artist into a box of their favorite tools. Trace and cut the top and bottom of the box. Cut two ³/₄"x4¹/₈" and ¹/₂"x2¹/₂" black strips and glue in the corners of the box bottom. Trim. Mat the top and bottom on black. Use your favorite colors or chose colors to coordinate with your photos and make six crayons. Finish with black details. Glue the bottom of the crayons to the bottom of the lid. Glue the bottom of the box over the lid. Crop and mat your photos and glue behind the crayons. Color this fun! Patterns on page 141.

- **patterned Paper Pizazz™:** yellow check, yellow dot (*Bright Tints*)
- **solid Paper Pizazz™:** black (*Solid Jewel Tones*); orange, fuschia, red, goldenrod, blue (*Plain Brights*)
- **alphabet template:** Frances Meyer, Inc.® Fat Caps
- **black pen:** Zig® Writer
- **white pen:** Pentel Milky Gel Roller
- **designer:** LeNae Gerig

No well-dressed lady goes anywhere without her purse as these two young elegant dressers show. LeNae agreed when she designed this winsome page. The blue stripe purse body was matted on black as was the blue diamond flap and handle. The gold "clasp" is matted on black and finished with black pen and a black 3/16" punched rectangle. The photos were matted on lavender and black with the journaling written directly on the flap. The perfect place to put your most important things! See inside the back cover for the patterns.

- **patterned Paper Pizazz™:** blue diamonds (*Soft Tints*); blue stripes (*Soft Tints,* also by the sheet)
- **specialty Paper Pizazz™:** metallic gold (*Metallic Papers,* also by the sheet)
- **solid Paper Pizazz™:** lavender (*Plain Pastels*); black (*Solid Jewel Tones*)
- **black pen:** Sakura Gelly Roll
- **designer:** LeNae Gerig

What better way to wrap up your Christmas photos and deliver them in style than in Santa's bag? The photos are glued to the Santa sack cut from burlap patterned paper and matted on black. Threading a red ribbon through slits cut at the bag neck and filling it with *Punch-Out™* toys help you finish this page in the twinkling of an eye. LeNae matted the photos on green then black. Cutting a 3/4"x3 3/8" green strip and matting it on black, she placed it over the top edge of the photo as the box lid. She glue a 3/8"x3/4" red strip in the center of the lid and added a punched bow outlined with black pen to finish the package. Gift tags matted on black journal the event. Pattern on page 143.

- **patterned Paper Pizazz™:** burlap (*Country,* also by the sheet)
- **solid Paper Pizazz™:** green, red (*Plain Brights*); white (*Plain Pastels*); black (*Solid Jewel Tones*)
- **Paper Pizazz™ Punch-Outs™:** toys (*Girls & Boys Punch-Outs™*)
- **7/8" bow punch:** McGill, Inc.
- **15" of 1/4" wide red satin ribbon:** C.M. Offray & Son, Inc.
- **X-Acto® knife, cutting surface**
- **black pen:** Zig® Millenium
- **designer:** LeNae Gerig

gift tag

When Alexis rocked her daddy to sleep, LeNae wrapped the photo in one big bear hug of everyone's favorite sleepy time toy. After matting the photo with a single pink mat, she cut the bear out of a sponged paper and matted all the pieces on black. LeNae glued the feet to the body, chalked the cheeks and ears then assembled the head. She positioned the photo on the bear's tummy and glued the arms over to "hold" it before gluing on the head. Isn't it a honey of a page? Patterns on page 144.

- **patterned Paper Pizazz™:** ivory sponged stars (*Spattered, Crackled & Sponged*)
- **solid Paper Pizazz™:** black (*Solid Jewel Tones*); pink (*Plain Pastels*)
- **pink decorative chalk:** Craf-T Products
- **black pen:** Zig® Writer
- **white pen:** Pentel Milky Gel Roller
- **designer:** LeNae Gerig

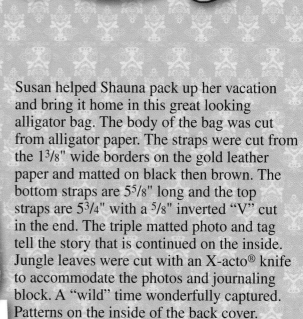

inside the page

Susan helped Shauna pack up her vacation and bring it home in this great looking alligator bag. The body of the bag was cut from alligator paper. The straps were cut from the 1³/₈" wide borders on the gold leather paper and matted on black then brown. The bottom straps are 5⁵/₈" long and the top straps are 5³/₄" with a ⁵/₈" inverted "V" cut in the end. The triple matted photo and tag tell the story that is continued on the inside. Jungle leaves were cut with an X-acto® knife to accommodate the photos and journaling block. A "wild" time wonderfully captured. Patterns on the inside of the back cover.

- **patterned Paper Pizazz™:** jungles leaves, gold leather with border (*Wild Things*); alligator (*Wild Things, also by the sheet*)
- **solid Paper Pizazz™:** brown, green, black (*Solid Jewel Tones*)
- **¹/₈" wide circle punch:** McGill, Inc.
- **15" length of natural raffia:** American Oak Preserving Co., Inc.
- **black pen:** Zig® Millenium
- **designer:** Susan Cobb

Meet one of the most versatile techniques in scrapbooking. Borders! They fill space, help tell stories, grow a page, and so much more! See what fabulous border ideas our designers (and not just our designers…scrapbookers just like you!) have developed. Punched to folded, layered to 3-D, simple to simply marvelous. Where are they going to take you?

We can give our children two things…
One is roots and the other is wings…

Summer 2001

Paper weaving—you did it in grade school and now it's a grown-up design technique as Arlene shows! She cut a $1\frac{1}{8}$"x11" strip of green paper with pattern-edged scissors and matted it on a $1\frac{1}{2}$" x11" white strip. She glued this $\frac{13}{16}$" from the left edge of the background paper. She then cut $1\frac{3}{4}$" squares of white and $\frac{3}{8}$" wide strips of the blue splatter and green sponged paper, weaving them over the white squares and gluing the ends to the back. She matted the woven squares on white and glued them evenly spaced along the "ribbon" on the left. Leaves punched from white and green paper were glued between the squares and on the squares as shown. The photo and journaling block were matted on green, white, blue splatter and white then glued to the green flourishes background paper. Definitely a dream weaver page, Arlene.

- **patterned Paper Pizazz™:** green flower, green sponged, blue splatter (*Soft and Subtle Textures*)
- **solid Paper Pizazz™:** green, white (*Plain Pastels*)
- **jumbo lace scallop scissors:** Family Treasures, Inc.
- **leaf punch:** Family Treasures, Inc.
- **designer:** Arlene Peterson

Light-hearted swirls romp on this bubbly page. Maddie's outfit inspired LeNae to use pink and lime green for the papers. She matted the photo on white, lime green, a wide pink swirl mat and lime green again. Positioning the photo to the right of the pink dot background left room for a border. Two $\frac{1}{4}$" wide white strips coordinate with the white journaling (and Maddie's bike). Large and small swirls were punched from the lime green and twirl merrily up and down the strips and as photo corners. A fun girl page.

- **patterned Paper Pizazz™:** pink dot, pink swirl (*Bright Tints*)
- **solid Paper Pizazz™:** lime green, white (*Plain Pastels*)
- **white alphabet stickers:** Making Memories™
- **small swirl, large swirl punches:** Marvy® Uchida
- **designer:** LeNae Gerig

Maddie

Our third place winner in the Spring Pages with Pizazz contest, Nicola Howard, made a sensational bordered page with two sheets of collage paper. She matted her photo on collage paper and then blue "velvet". She cut a 7$\frac{1}{2}$"x10$\frac{1}{2}$" section from one sheet of the collage paper, saving the floral elements. After matting it with vellum swirl paper, she positioned it to the right on the second sheet of collage paper. She cut out the flower and leaves from the first sheet and matted them on the blue "velvet" before positioning them over a "ribbon" of $\frac{1}{2}$" wide collage and $\frac{3}{8}$" wide vellum swirl. Blue "velvet" paper journaling letters and vellum cut-out raindrops finish the page. A marvelous shower of ideas, Nicola.

- **patterned Paper Pizazz™:** green/blue botanical (*Collage Papers*); blue velvet (*"Velvet" Backgrounds*)
- **specialty Paper Pizazz™:** vellum swirls (*Vellum Papers*, by the sheet)
- **Paper Pizazz™ Cut-Outs™:** raindrops (*Vellum Cut-Outs™*)
- **white pen:** Pentel Milky Gel Roller
- **silver pen:** Pentech Fireworks Gel Roller
- **designer:** Nicola Howard

The floral 3-D effect is utterly charming on this wedding page. Amy used fancy knifework to trim a 3" wide strip of ivy leaves from the ivy paper and matted it in black. She cut out individual leaves and matted them on black, along with individual pink roses matted on black. These were attached with foam tape to the ivy border to raise them. The photos were triple matted in black and white and the journaling blocks in black, white and pink roses. Arranging all the elements on the page before gluing allows for overlapping the border.

- **patterned Paper Pizazz™:** blue suede (*Heritage Papers*, also by the sheet); ivy, pink roses (by the sheet)
- **solid Paper Pizazz™:** black (*Solid Jewel Tones*); white (*Plain Pastels*)
- **X-acto® knife, cutting surface:** Hunt Mfg.
- **foam mounting tape:** Scotch® Brand
- **designers:** Amy Gustafson and LeNae Gerig

Wainscoating is a marvelous technique to use for making a page with one photo. Shauna chose a white with blue speckles paper for the background, then used ½ sheet of blue and white stripe to cover the lower part of the page. A matching checked border and embellishments neatly finish the border. She matted the photo in white and on a coordinating green. Pen work duplicates the pattern in the stripe paper. When you plan a page using wainscoating—think of your page as a wall for balancing your elements.

- **patterned Paper Pizazz™:** white with blue specks, blue/white stripe, check border, heart and star cut-outs (*Lisa Williams Blue, Yellow & Green*)
- **solid Paper Pizazz™:** white, green (*Plain Pastels*)
- **black pen:** Zig® Writer
- **designer:** Shauna Berglund-Immel

Frosty papers and icy snowflakes gave us a shiver of excitement when we saw Teri Cutts winning page for the Winter Pages with Pizazz content. Teri created a quadrant background using ice blues, silver and vellum. She quadruple matted the photo and angled it for more visual interest. The journaling banners echo the papers while die-cut snowflakes covered with tiny clear marbles float down. But it's the border adrift in folded snowflakes that makes this page such a cool choice. Using blues, silver and vellum, Teri takes us to a winter wonderland. Snowflake instructions on page 140.

- **patterned Paper Pizazz™:** blue frost, blue ripple (*Great Backgrounds*)
- **specialty Paper Pizazz™:** silver (*Heavy Metal Papers*); snowflake vellum (*Vellum Papers*)
- **solid Paper Pizazz™:** dark blue (*Solid Jewel Tones*); white (*Plain Pastels*)
- **snowflake die-cuts:** Stamping Station
- **tiny clear marbles:** Halcraft USA, Inc.
- **pinking scissors:** Fiskars®, Inc.
- **designer:** Teri Cutts

Tiffany Bodily's honorable mention winner of the Spring Pages with Pizazz contest blossoms with a wonderful border. Tiffany used pattern-edged scissors to create the grass edge and the wide wave border. She matted a 2" wide lavender strip on purple and centered it over the swirl as a "bed" for her flowers. Using a template, she picked a bouquet of colors and patterns to coordinate with the photos. Layering the matted elements builds depth in the border. A definite pick of the crop!

- **patterned Paper Pizazz™:** blue dot, purple swirl, green plaid, pink floral, yellow stripe (*Soft Tints*)
- **solid Paper Pizazz™:** purple, green (*Solid Jewel Tones*); green, lavender (*Solid Muted Colors*)
- **large swirl punch:** Family Treasures, Inc.
- **1¼" circle punch:** Memories Forever
- **1" circle punch:** McGill, Inc.
- **grass wide scissors:** Fiskars®, Inc.
- **wave big cuts scissors:** Provo Craft®
- **fun flowers designer template:** Provo Craft®
- **black pens:** Zig® Writer
- **designer:** Tiffany Bodily

The Spring Pages with Pizazz contest brought another honorable mention winning border page by Kimberly Llorens. Beginning with a pink/purple/yellow muted background matching Amanda's dress, Kimberly matted her photo on pink vellum and peach/pink/yellow muted patterned papers matching the tulips. She punch rectangle holes around the mat and wove in paper raffia tied at the corners before matting on pink and lavender. She cropped a photo of the tulips into four 1¼" squares and matted each on pink/peach/yellow muted and then lavender. A field of beauties, Kimberly!

- **patterned Paper Pizazz™:** pink/purple/yellow muted, peach/pink/yellow muted (*Great Backgrounds*)
- **specialty Paper Pizazz™:** pink vellum (*Pastel Vellum Papers*)
- **solid Paper Pizazz™:** pink, lavender (*Plain Pastels*)
- **¹⁄₁₆" wide rectangle punch:** Fiskars®, Inc.
- **1¼" square punch:** Family Treasures, Inc.
- **designer:** Kimberly Llorens

When working with heritage photos, it's easy to use black, white and gray paper but you can use so much more and still be respectful of the photo. Let's see some ideas…

LeNae recommends taking an element from your black & white heritage photos then translating it into color as a great way to find a theme for your page. The hydrangeas in the forefront of this photo set the tone for this beautiful page. LeNae matted a purple stripe on purple and then centered it on the hydrangea background. The photo was copied and trimmed with pattern-edged scissors for the vintage snapshot effect before matting it on black. The black photo corners are reminiscent of old photo albums. Hydrangea borders trimmed with a bow finish this gentle memory.

- **patterned Paper Pizazz**™: hydrangeas (*Watercolor Florals*); purple stripe (*Soft Tints*)
- **solid Paper Pizazz**™: purple, black (*Solid Jewel Tones*)
- **Paper Pizazz**™ **Punch-Outs**™: hydrangea borders (*Watercolor Punch-Outs*™)
- **black photo corners:** Canson-Talens, Inc.
- **deckle scissors:** Family Treasures, Inc.
- **9" of 1/4" wide lavender satin ribbon:** C.M. Offray & Son, Inc.
- **white pen:** Pentel Milky Gel Roller
- **designer:** LeNae Gerig

You can practically hear the band playing "Anchors Away" when LeNae runs up the flags on this page saluting a family's own hero. Red, white and blue were a natural selection. The heritage photo was matted five times with narrow solid mats separating the wide red and blue patterned mats. Triangles (see pattern) were cut, matted on black paper and placed on a 1/4" wide white strip. The punched stars are outlined with black pen on both the flags and the journaling block. A 21-gun salute for this page.

- **patterned Paper Pizazz**™: blue stripe with black and red border, blue with white dots (*Heritage Papers*); red with stars (*Coordinating Colors*™ *Red & White*); red and white stripe (*Ho,Ho, Ho!!!*, also by the sheet)
- **solid Paper Pizazz**™: black (*Solid Jewel Tones*); white (*Plain Pastel*)
- **1/2" wide star punch:** Marvy® Uchida
- **black pen:** Zig® Writer
- **designer:** LeNae Gerig

A little girl stares out from another time…so very feminine in her lacy dress and oversize hair bow. Shauna was enchanted with the photo and wanted to design a page befitting such a proper young lady. She chose a tone-on-tone flourishes background reminiscent of a time-faded wallpaper. The photo was matted with white, black and vintage lace as was the journaling block. Almost perfect but it still needed something more. A parasol, lacy pair of gloves and high-button shoes cut from vintage looking papers and lightly chalked to "age" them became tender reminders of this little girl's world. Forever young. Patterns for the boots and gloves on page 143.

- **patterned Paper Pizazz™:** vintage lace (*Heritage Papers, Making Heritage Scrapbook Pages*, also by the sheet); tone-on-tone flourishes (*Heritage Papers*); black with white dot (*Making Heritage Scrapbook Pages*, also by the sheet); white moiré (by the sheet)
- **solid Paper Pizazz™:** black (*Solid Jewel Tones*); white (*Plain Pastels*)
- **small Victorian boot, small glove, small parasol die-cuts:** Accu/Cut® Systems
- **brown, black, white decorative chalks:** Craf-T Products
- **scallop scissors:** Fiskars®, Inc.
- **foam mounting tape:** Scotch® Brand
- **black pen:** Sakura Gelly Roll
- **designer:** Shauna Berglund-Immel

Torn papers in muted colors give a soft time-worn look to heritage pages. LeNae chose three vintage looking papers for this page. She tore blocks of the plaid and peach flower papers to form a background behind the photo. Torn ivory and plaid strips form a "ribbon" on the right side of the page for the torn journaling hearts and envelope embellishment. To make the envelope, tear a 2¹/₂"x7¹/₂" strip of paper and then tear the top into a point. Fold the paper into thirds with the point on the bottom fold.

When tearing papers, LeNae says you can use two methods. Placing a ruler on the line where you want the tear and pulling up on the paper will produce even lines like those on the ivory photo mats. Freehand tearing produces irregular shapes and raggedy lines. Use your fingers as a guide and make short smooth tears for this effect, she advises.

- **patterned Paper Pizazz™:** peach floral, peach/ yellow plaid, peach flower (*Mixing Soft Patterned Papers*)
- **solid Paper Pizazz™:** 12"x12" ivory (*Solid Pastel Papers*)
- **straight metal-edge ruler**
- **6" of ¹/₄" wide peach satin ribbon:** C.M. Offray & Son, Inc.
- **black pen:** Zig® Millenium
- **designer:** LeNae Gerig

Album pages can be "grown" but did you know they can be "shrunk"? Shauna loved the effect of the 8½"x11" heritage butterflies over the 12"x12" purple flower collage paper. To fit them, she used a light box and positioned the purple flowers over the vellum page and traced around the border of the vellum paper and cut out a perfect fit. She used knifework to cut the left wing on all the blue butterflies in the border and both wings in the butterfly in the right corner. She then outlined both the wing and the cut-out edge in gold. She matted the photo on gold, purple vellum, purple flower collage and blue vellum. She outlined the edge of both vellums with the gold pen and then glued the matted photo to the front and the collage paper to the back of the vellum paper. A gentle reflection of the past.

- **patterned Paper Pizazz™**: purple flower (*Collage Papers*)
- **specialty Paper Pizazz™**: butterflies (*Heritage Vellum*); lavender, lavender blue (*Pastel Vellum Papers*); gold (*Metallic Papers*)
- **gold pen**: Sakura Gelly Roll
- **designer**: Shauna Berglund-Immel

Shauna creates a beautiful tribute in these pages. She chose the heritage floral borders and a purple sponged background paper. Selecting a collage of photos, she edged each with a ¹/₁₆" strip of brown outline with black in keeping with the twig border on the vellum paper. They were placed on the sponged background so they fall in line with the border of the vellum flowers. The floral vellum is glued on top. She took the color memorial photo and placed it in a brown "twig" frame tied with gold metallic thread and positioned it on the vellum paper. The journaling and the photos tell a loving story of a grandmother's life.

- **patterned Paper Pizazz™**: purple sponged (*Pretty Papers*)
- **specialty Paper Pizazz™**: vellum floral borders (*Heritage Vellum*)
- **solid Paper Pizazz™**: brown (*Solid Muted Tones*)
- **metallic gold thread**: Westrim® Crafts
- **black pen**: Sakura Gelly Roll
- **designer**: Shauna Berglund-Immel

Many heritage photos are like the one used in this page…only a person with no telling details. LeNae called on a variety of techniques to tell the story of this photo. She chose the letters paper, tearing and burning the sheet to age it. She used the same technique on a smaller piece of "handmade" ivory and then tore a sheet of tan vellum and layered all on the background paper. She matted the photo on ivory and used pattern-edged scissors before matting it on black and adding photo corners. She photocopied a relevant stamp, matted it on black and added the stamped sealing wax embellishment. The journaling block was cut in the shape of a tag and "aged" with chalking. Two die-cut keys are attached with gold thread to unlock these memories.

- **patterned Paper Pizazz™:** letters (*Black & White Photos,* also by the sheet); 12"x12" gold with black border (by the sheet); ivory handmade (*The "Handmade" Look*)
- **specialty Paper Pizazz™:** specialty gold, specialty copper (*Metallic Papers,* also by the sheet); tan vellum (*Pastel Vellum*)
- **solid Paper Pizazz™:** black (*Solid Jewel Tones*); ivory (*Plain Pastels*)
- **1/8" and 1/4" hole punches:** McGill, Inc.
- **key die-cut:** Accu/Cut® Systems
- **deckle scissors:** Family Treasures, Inc.
- **brown decorative chalk:** Craf-T Products
- **6" of metallic gold thread:** Westrim® Crafts
- **gold photo corners:** Canson-Talens, Inc.
- **black pen:** Zig® Writer
- **designer:** LeNae Gerig

LeNae recreated the room where these children had their photo taken for this page. She chose a blue/purple brushed background paper matching a portion of the background in the photo. She teamed it with a coordinating floral echoing the roses in the shawl. She trimmed the brushed paper to 10"x11³/4" and the floral paper to 2"x10". She glued them together before gluing them centered on a 10¹/8"x11³/4" lavender paper and then to a 12"x12" purple. She matted the photo on white, trimmed with pattern-edged scissors. She cut a 10" strip of laser lace and glued it over the seam of the background paper with another ¹/2"x10" lace border glued to the bottom of the page. Two ¹/2"x11" strips of laser lace were glued along the sides. An old-fashion buggy vellum embellishment completed this page. A charming "home" for this heritage photo.

- **patterned Paper Pizazz™:** blue/purple brushed, blue floral (*Mixing Heritage Papers*)
- **specialty Paper Pizazz™:** laser lace (*Romantic Papers,* also by the sheet); baby carriage (*Heritage Vellum*)
- **solid Paper Pizazz™:** 12"x12" white, lavender (*Solid Pastel Papers*); 12"x12" purple (*Coordinating Colors™ Purple & Blue*)
- **mini antique Victorian scissors:** Family Treasures, Inc.
- **oval templates:** *Paper Flair™ Windows #2*
- **black pen:** Zig™ Millenium
- **designer:** LeNae Gerig

A marvelous way to tell the story of your page is to photograph signs and then use them in your layout. It's the perfect technique for travel pages. But don't stop there! Think of other moments when a sign can tell the story for you—a marquee for a special concert or a banner at a party. Let's see how it's done!

Arlene rocks on this page. Choosing her colors from the plane and tarmac, she began with a red with hollow dot background. She matted 1¹/₄" blue star borders on 1¹/₂" black borders and placed black triangles in opposite corners. Punched stars and music notes keep the rhythm going as the photos rock down the page where the silhouette cut, black matted sign tells it like it was. The legend lives on.

- **patterned Paper Pizazz™:** blue stars (by the sheet); red with hollow dot (*Bold & Bright*)
- **solid Paper Pizazz™:** red (*Plain Brights*); black (*Solid Jewel Tones*)
- **music note, 1" wide star punches:** McGill, Inc.
- **³/₈" wide star punch:** Family Treasures, Inc.
- **Border Buddy™ template:** Frances Meyer, Inc.®
- **designer:** Arlene Peterson

Scenery photos can get mixed over time—was that Yellowstone or Yosemite? LeNae says to snap a photo of signs and use them to build a scenic page. Here, she captures the season and the location with the fall leaves background paper and the black matted fall gold paper. A simple brown mat coordinates the photos with the background and maintains the rustic simplicity of the photos. Cropping the park sign and matting it on black makes it easy to read. Now you'll know exactly where you are when traveling the memory highway.

- **patterned Paper Pizazz™:** 12"x12" fall leaves (by the sheet); fall leaves with pumpkin (*Bj's Gold & Handpainted Papers*)
- **solid Paper Pizazz™:** brown, black (*Solid Jewel Tones*)
- **black pen:** Zig® Writer
- **designer:** LeNae Gerig

LeNae actually takes us on her trip in this page by recreating the feel of New Orleans, a city famous for its hidden gardens. She began with a brick patterned paper, trimming it to 4"x12". She cut a strip of 1" wide brick, matted it on black and used foam tape to give the feel of the brick overhang. She selected a garden paper and positioned it with the flowers showing behind the wall. She trimmed the top of the paper so the page remained 12"x12". Photos were matted on white and finished with blue decorative chalk making them look sky-mounted. The story of the cropped, black matted tiled sign on the "brick wall" is explained in the journaling block. Hmmm, smell the magnolias!

- **patterned Paper Pizazz™:** 12"x12" brick wall (by the sheet); flower garden (*Watercolor Backgrounds*)
- **solid Paper Pizazz™:** 12"x12" black (*12"x12" Coordinating Colors™ Black & White*); white (*Plain Pastels*)
- **deckle scissors:** Family Treasures, Inc.
- **blue decorative chalk:** Craf-T Products
- **foam mounting tape:** Scotch® Brand
- **designer:** LeNae Gerig

Arlene uses her sign to create a setting for her photos. After matting the sign on brown paper, she made "posts" to hold it. She cut four ³/4" wide strips of barnwood patterned paper, rounded the corners by trimming, matted them on brown and added black pen work to age them. She covered the bottom half of the clouds background paper with the sandstone paper matted at the top with a ¹/4" wide brown strip. She added individual stones cut from the beach pebbles patterned paper. The photos were matted on teal to match the sign and then black. By placing the city street shot above and the beach photos below the sandstone paper, Arlene gives us the feel of this oceanside town.

- **patterned Paper Pizazz™:** clouds (*Vacation*, also by the sheet); sandstone, beach pebbles, barnwood (by the sheet)
- **solid Paper Pizazz™:** brown, teal, black (*Solid Jewel Tones*)
- **deckle scissors:** Fiskars®, Inc.
- **designer:** Arlene Peterson

No where is it written that album pages have to be flat. Some pages just cry out for accessories—buttons, bows, wire, a souvenier, charms, whatever your imagination can conjure. Study the pages our designers have created and then start collecting your own wardrobe of embellishments.

Shauna illuminates the moment when a young dancer is dreaming of her future. The photo is matted on copper catching the light in Brooke's hair and lacy mesh to echo her tulle dress then placed on a daydreamy collage background. But it's the beautiful paper tutu that tells the story. Using pink moiré paper as the base, she layered a second skirt in the mesh paper and a third in pink vellum. Shauna outlined it in white pen, glued ribbon around the waist, added a sheer pink bow, vellum flowers and hung it on a copper wire "hanger". Vellum journaling blocks outlined in copper pen and journaled in white complete a tender "someday" page. Dress and hanger patterns on page 142.

- **patterned Paper Pizazz™:** pink/purple collage (*Collage Papers*); pink moiré (by the sheet)
- **specialty Paper Pizazz™:** copper (*Metallic Papers*, also by the sheet); lacy mesh (*Lacy Vellum*); plum pink vellum, dark pink vellum (*Pastel Vellum Papers*)
- **Paper Pizazz™ Cut-Outs™:** flowers (*Lacy Vellum Cut-Outs™*)
- **dress die-cut:** Accu/Cut® Systems
- **copper wire:** Artistic Wire, Ltd.™
- **copper pen:** Zebra Jimnie Gel Roller
- **white pen:** Pentel Milky Gel Roller
- **9" of ⁵/₈" wide pink sheer ribbon:** Sheer Creations
- **2" of ¹/₄" wide white satin ribbon:** C.M. Offray & Son, Inc.
- **designer:** Shauna Berglund-Immel

Button, button, who's got the button? Arlene does on this gentle outdoor page. She chose a family of papers mirroring the muted feel of the overcast day. She took the blue from Alyshia's clothes as her "Golden Rule" color. Strips of ⁷/₈" wide pattern paper were matted on blue and arranged in a frame around the center photo. 1³/₄" squares of patterned paper matted on blue were centered with punched flowers. Natural color buttons become the flower centers and accent the photo frame. A simple touch that buttons this page up just right.

- **patterned Paper Pizazz™:** yellow stripe, yellow flower, green diamond, green flourishes (*Mixing Soft Patterned Papers*)
- **solid Paper Pizazz™:** blue (*Plain Brights*); white (*Plain Pastels*)
- **1¹/₄" flower punch:** Family Treasures, Inc.
- **⁵/₈" wide and ³/₈" wide natural color buttons:** Coats & Clark
- **designer:** Arlene Peterson

"Look to the photo for inspiration" is Shauna's advice and what she did in this adorable page. After matting Kaelin's photo on gold and denim, she made a denim pocket complete with an official looking tag, positioned it over the photos and glued the edges. Shauna created an overall strap with denim paper, copper wire and a gold button. She formed the strap adjuster and slipped it over and up the paper. She attached the hook, glued the paper under and then glued the button onto the paper. Pen "stitches" make the denim paper look sewn. A strand of tiny faux pearls trails out of the pocket. "Overall", it's absolutely marvelous! Pocket pattern is on page 143.

- **patterned Paper Pizazz™:** denim (*Country*, also by the sheet); blue/purple sponged (by the sheet)
- **specialty Paper Pizazz™:** gold (*Metallic Papers*, also by the sheet)
- **solid Paper Pizazz™:** white (*Plain Pastels*)
- **copper wire:** Artistic Wire, Ltd.
- **3mm pearl strand:** Wrights®
- **3/4" gold button:** Coats & Clark
- **foam mounting tape:** Scotch® Brand
- **black pen:** Sakura Gelly Roll
- **photography:** I.N.V.U. Portraits by Helen
- **designer:** Shauna Berglund-Immel

A beautifully composed page does not have to be complicated. It just needs the right accent as Arlene shows here. She matted the photo on lavender then a wide mat of patterned paper, lavender and white. Note how she places the photo closer to the top, leaving room for a special touch. Here she layered sheer lavender, satin-edged sheer lavender, and pink satin ribbons before weaving them through the mat and finishing with a bow. It ties up this cute page perfectly.

- **patterned Paper Pizazz™:** lavender flowers, white flowers (*Lisa Williams Pink, Lavender & Beige*)
- **solid Paper Pizazz™:** white, lavender (*Plain Pastels*)
- **1/2" square punch:** Marvy® Uchida
- **14" each of 7/8" wide sheer lavender, 1/4" wide lavender satin edge sheer, 1/8" wide pink satin ribbons:** C.M. Offray & Son, Inc.
- **designer:** Arlene Peterson

Heritage pages are wonderful places to use embellishments. Shauna layered blue "family" vellum over a 12"x12" letters background paper. She trimmed the title from the rose "memories" vellum and matted it on gold then black. After triple matting the photo with black and gold, she chronicles youthful activities with the help of an assortment of charms. 1 3/4" squares of rose vellum cut from the unused part of the "memories" page are journaled and an appropriate embellishment tied with metallic gold thread then glued to each square. What else can you call this page but charming?

- **patterned Paper Pizazz™:** letters (*For Black & White Photos*)
- **specialty Paper Pizazz™:** blue family vellum, rose memories vellum (*Heritage Vellum*), gold (*Metallic Papers*, also by the sheet)
- **solid Paper Pizazz™:** black (*Solid Jewel Tones*)
- **1 3/4" square punch:** Marvy® Uchida
- **gold charms:** Creative Beginnings
- **metallic gold thread:** Westrim® Crafts
- **black pen:** Sakura Gelly Roll
- **designer:** Shauna Berglund-Immel

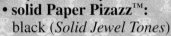

The stars come out to celebrate this page! The photos set the colors for this page and Arlene followed with blue and yellow matting placed on a blue with sponged yellow stars and moons background paper. She cut a star-shaped journaling block and made yellow and blue border strips. She strung 1/2" star-shaped beads on yellow craft wire, coiling the wire to hold the beads in position. To coil, wrap the wire around a pencil, then slip off. The beads and wire were glued to the borders and around the journaling star. A celestial treat!

- **patterned Paper Pizazz™:** blue with sponged moon and stars (by the sheet)
- **solid Paper Pizazz™:** yellow (*Plain Pastels*); teal (*Solid Jewel Tones*)
- **star #2 die-cut:** Accu/Cut® Systems
- **1/2" wide blue, gold, clear sparkle beads:** The Beadery
- **36" of yellow wire:** Artistic Wire Ltd.
- **designer:** Arlene Peterson

What a super cute idea! LeNae wanted to sum up her baby shower so she snapped photos of several of the outfits. She created the background by trimming 3^1/$_2$" off the plaid paper with patterned-edged scissors. She added a 1"x12" strip of light green and trimmed the paper again with the patterned-edged scissors before gluing it to the clouds patterned paper. She glued a ^{1}/$_4$"x12" strip of pink ^{1}/$_8$" below the scallop edge. The photos were matted on pink and green then detailed with pen work as was the pink strip. LeNae cut out the three baby sleepers and matted them on green then strung ribbon across the clouds and "hung" them with mini clothespins. Baby themed Punch-Outs™ provided instant journaling blocks. A definite special delivery!

- **patterned Paper Pizazz™:** 12"x12" clouds (*Our Vacation*, also by the sheet), green/pink plaid (*Baby's First Year*, also by the sheet)
- **solid Paper Pizazz™:** 12"x12" pink, light green (*Solid Pastel Papers*)
- **Paper Pizazz™ Punch-Outs™:** shoe, heart, pacifier, rattle (*Baby Punch-Outs™*)
- **seagull scissors:** Fiskars®, Inc.
- **six 1" long spring clothespins:** Forster Mfg. Inc.
- **14" of ^{1}/$_8$" wide white satin ribbon:** C.M. Offray & Son, Inc.
- **black pen:** Sakura Gelly Roll
- **designer:** LeNae Gerig

Shauna takes us for a walk in the woods with this amazing page. Beginning with a green diamond collage background paper, she cut ^{1}/$_4$"x11" strips of blue vellum and placed them between the diamonds with brown eyelets. She matted the photo on blue vellum and a torn "handmade" beige paper. She then placed it on a rectangle of green vellum and attached it to the background with eyelets in the folded corners. Shauna tied a 6" piece twine into a knot, threaded it through an eyelet on the photo and then to a eyelet in the background, securing it on the back before tucking the skeleton leaves under the photo. She made a journaling block by layering 2^1/$_2$"x7" green vellum and fern vellum. She wrapped the top around a small twig and fastened it with brown eyelets. She glued the top of the journaling block and used eyelets to attach the bottom corners. This marvelous page really takes flight!

- **patterned Paper Pizazz™:** green diamond collage (*Collage Papers*); "handmade" beige ("*Handmade*" *Papers*)
- **specialty Paper Pizazz™:** sage green vellum, blue vellum (*Pastel Vellum Papers*); fern vellum (*Vellum Papers*, also available by the sheet)
- **brown and green eyelets:** AmericanPin/HyGlo
- **bronze and gold skeleton leaves:** Black Ink Decorative Accents
- **black pen:** Sakura Gelly Roll
- **designer:** Shauna Berglund-Immel

"A stitch in time makes your page look just fine" says Arlene. She proves it by letting embroidery floss whip together the fun elements on this page. She matted two photos on one pink vellum mat and stitched a running line of green embroidery thread. After matting the photo on a pink posy and green vellum, she used a pink embroidery thread in the running stitch border. Green and pink hearts in various sizes and patterns were punch and arranged randomly down the page. Arlene placed a $4^1/2$" strip of pink vellum over the hearts and stitched it to the background paper with the green embroidery floss. Pink embroidery floss finishes the two hearts around the journaling. This page is "sew" super, Arlene.

- **patterned Paper Pizazz™**: pink swirl, pink check, pink posy, green stripe, green check, green flower (*Soft Tints*)
- **specialty Paper Pizazz™**: pink vellum, green vellum (*Pastel Vellum Papers*)
- $1/2$", $3/4$" $1^1/4$" and 3" wide heart punches: Marvy® Uchida
- **green and pink embroidery floss**: DMC Corp.
- **green pen**: Zebra Jimnie Gel Roller
- **designer**: Arlene Peterson

The sparkle of the Christmas season is joyously reflected in these pages. Shauna first "grew" an $8^1/2$"x11" page by layering gold matted holiday paper on a 12"x12" green "velvet" background paper. She matted the photos and journaling blocks on gold and green. Then she added the glow with tiny gold marbles. Using double sided adhesive sheets, she die-cut journaling letters and six $1/2$" squares. She pressed the cut adhesive into the tiny marbles and attached them to the letters and squares. The letters are positioned as shown and the squares went over diamonds in the red background paper (bottom row three right of holly and three left of jolly). The spirit of Christmas past lovingly preserved.

- **patterned Paper Pizazz™**: holly leaves on red diamonds (*Bj's Gold & Handpainted Papers*)
- **specialty Paper Pizazz™**: gold (*Metallic Papers*, also by the sheet)
- **solid Paper Pizazz™**: green, red (*Solid Muted Colors*); white (*Plain Pastels*)
- $1/2$" square punch: McGill, Inc.
- **traveler alphabet die-cuts**: Accu/Cut® Systerms
- **metallic gold tiny glass marbles**: Halcraft USA, Inc.
- **double sided high tack adhesive sheet**: Embossing Essentials
- **designer**: Shauna Berglund-Immel

Everybody knows when scrapbookers get together it's going to be lots of fun. Shauna's page catches all the love and fun scrappers bring to their work. She layered yellow stripe and white papers over blue gingham paper, securing them with yellow eyelets for the background. The photo was matted on white and red. She attached it with white eyelets, using extra eyelets along the bottom to use for the ribbon dangles. A delightful trick was using white eyelets to form the holes in the title letters cut from blue dot paper and matted on white. She strung a ribbon through the eyelets on the photo, hanging 2"x3" rectangles of yellow vellum outlined with white pen and featuring a scrappy little sticker. They were then topped with a punched red hearts centered with white eyelets. A red heart swings merrily from ribbon strung through the "a". A page to reflect the spirit and joy of scrappers everywhere!

- **patterned Paper Pizazz™:** blue dots (*12"x12" Soft Tints*); blue gingham, yellow stripes (*12"x12" Soft Tints*, also by the sheet)
- **specialty Paper Pizazz™:** yellow vellum (*Pastel Vellum Papers*)
- **solid Paper Pizazz™:** white (*Solid Pastel Papers*); red (*Plain Brights*)
- **1¼" heart punch:** Marvy® Uchida
- **Paper Pizazz™ stickers:** scrapbook friends (*Annie Lang's School Time*)
- **lettering template:** EK Success® ABC Tracers™
- **15" of ⅛" wide white satin ribbon:** C.M. Offray & Son, Inc.
- **½" wide red heart bead:** Westrim® Crafts
- **yellow and white eyelets:** Stamp Studio
- **white pen:** Pentel Milky Gel Roller
- **black pen:** Sakura Gelly Roll
- **designer:** Shauna Berglund-Immel

Lisa hung the Jones family on their tree in style. She created the appropriate setting with green vellum "grass" over a blue chalked sky. A brown suede die-cut tree was centered on the page with chalked punched vellum leaves drifting over the landscape. Each photo was easily framed using frame Punch-Outs™ and hung with copper wire from the tree. A tin plaque was mounted with foam tape on a marble paper and hung on the tree with wire. A tiny punched flower covers the end of the wire. Die-cut letters were matted on brown suede positioned along the bottom of the page. One classy family, Lisa!

- **patterned Paper Pizazz™:** brown marble, brown suede (*For Black & White Photos,* also by the sheet)
- **specialty Paper Pizazz™:** green vellum, white vellum (*12"x12" Pastel Vellum Papers,* also by the sheet)
- **solid Paper Pizazz™:** white (*Plain Pastels*), black (*Solid Jewel Tones*)
- **Paper Pizazz™ Punch-Outs™:** frames (*Charms Punch-Outs™*)
- **1" wide and 1/2" wide maple leaf punches:** Marvy® Uchida
- **1" long elm leaf punches:** McGill, Inc.
- **tree and 1¼" long traveler letter die-cuts:** Accu/Cut® Systems
- **yellow, red, brown, orange, green decorative chalks:** Craf-T Products
- **deckle scissors:** Family Treasures, Inc.
- **20-gauge & 22-gauge copper wire:** Artistic Wire Ltd.
- **oval rusty tin plaque:** Westwater® Enterprises
- **designer:** Lisa Garcia-Bergstedt

Layer it!

My phone is
my life!
Hannah, Cristy & me
talking to Jen
Summer 2001

KRISTIN
JUNE
2001

string a garland!

Create a plaid!

Lazy,
hazy, crazy days
of
Summer
Jennifer 2001

I love vellum, but what can I DO WITH IT?

make a quilt block!

It's true…everybody does love vellum. Who wouldn't?

Beautiful as they are alone, they are the magic transforming an album page from special to spectacular. You'll reach for vellum again and again after seeing what wonderful things can be done with it.

We begin showing you the best ways to attach vellum to your pages. Securing it without glue showing through can be a problem but we'll offer up ways to hide it.

Stained glass and painted vellums add the look of art to pages. Layer it, cut it apart, turn it on its head…you'll never run out of possibilities. Painted vellum Cut-Outs™ let you place a glowing spot of color anywhere.

White-on-white and tone-on-tone vellums soften and enhance any background with their light touch. But when you need a bright splash of color, our colored vellums are just the ticket.

Lacy vellums add a whisper of pattern to your page. Metallic vellums scatter gold dust, shimmering in rich patterns.

Backgrounds to mats, embellishments to journaling blocks, vellum is so versatile you'll never run out of ways to use it.

Warning: Vellum is very brittle and any creases will leave a permanent mark. Be careful when purchasing vellum by the sheet to keep it flat. Buying a vellum collection in a book will help protect your purchase and give you a vellum collection to play with. A final warning, vellum is very addictive—in a fun sort of way!

The big question is how to attach vellum without the glue showing. Here's how to make your vellum stay put and still look beautiful.

Hide the glue #1—The most basic technique is to place the glue so it's hidden under another element on your page. For example, glue the photo to a vellum mat and then pick up the matted photo and only put glue behind the photo before attaching it to the background. Leave the edges unglued.

Hide the glue #2—When using vellum that has a design, place glue **only** under the design—that might be painted, stained glass, metallic or lacy vellum.

Layer by layer #3—When using multiple layers of vellum under a photo or journaling block, begin by gluing the **top** element to the next piece. Continue through the elements positioning the glue behind the photo to hide it, and finishing by gluing the bottom layer to the background paper. Remember, you don't have to glue down every inch of vellum for it to stick!

There's no where to hide—If you absolutely have to glue the vellum and there is no place to hide it, then use the thinnest possible line of dry glue close to the edge. We prefer a dry glue stick (acid-free, of course) and we find it's best to put glue on the paper rather than the vellum. You can mask a glue line by edging the vellum with a pen.

Don't use glue—There are many ways to attach vellum to your page without using glue. Use eyelets or brads. Punch holes and tie it on with a ribbon or raffia. Sew it on with needle and thread. Photo corners can be used effectively to hold the vellum or cover glue in the corners.

Stained glass vellum is a beautiful addition to any page but is a real natural with these church photos. Shauna chose a blue/purple sponged background paper. She matted the main photo on white and then on black using a geometric border punch to create a tracery around the photo. She glued lavender blue vellum behind the photo and placed it high on the background. She created a vellum pocket by trimming the floral stained glass vellum to $8^1/2"x5"$ and gluing it on the lower part of the page. She slipped the baptism announcement in the pocket and added a small white and black matted photo to the front. An inspired page, Shauna.

- **patterned Paper Pizazz™:** blue/purple sponged (by the sheet)
- **specialty Paper Pizazz™:** floral stained glass vellum (*Stained Glass Vellum*); lavender blue (*Pastel Vellum Papers*)
- **solid Paper Pizazz™:** black (*Solid Jewel Tones*); white (*Plain Pastels*)
- **geometric border punch:** Family Treasures, Inc.
- **black pen:** Sakura Gelly Roll
- **designer:** Shauna Berglund-Immel

One inspiration led to another in this gorgeous page from Shauna. Matching the waterfall in the stained glass mountain border to the waterfall behind the heritage photo started the ideas flowing. She matted the vellum over the clouds background paper creating a wonderful overall watery effect. She then tore strips of plain pastel vellum papers and layered them to match the sky behind the stained glass mountain. The vellum journal block is embellished with two leaf clusters matching the stained glass tree. The black and white photo stands out against the glorious burst of colors throughout this page.

- **patterned Paper Pizazz™:** clouds (*Vacation #2*, also by the sheet)
- **specialty Paper Pizazz™:** yellow vellum, orange vellum, peach vellum, pink vellum, plum vellum, blue violet vellum, blue vellum, green vellum (*Pastel Vellum Papers*)
- **solid Paper Pizazz™:** black (*Solid Jewel Tones*)
- **oval die-cut:** Ellison® Craft & Design
- **black pen:** Sakura Gelly Roll
- **designer:** Shauna Berglund-Immel

oval ©&™ Ellison® Craft & Design

Beautiful "hand-painted" designs on a translucent sheet of vellum will have you snapping photos just to be able to try all the wonderful possibilities. Whether you cut out the designs or use the whole sheet, you'll love the artistry painted vellum brings to your pages.

One way to use painted vellum is to cut it apart! Arlene chose the garden pattern to finish the story on this page. After matting the photo and journaling block on white, green chevron and white, she placed them on a green stripe background. She cut out the lattice/wheelbarrow border, trimming it closely. She cut the motif apart, placing the lattice with ivy along the edge of the photo overlapping slightly. The wheelbarrow and remaining lattice were positioned in the corner overlapping the journaling block. A garden fresh page.

- **patterned Paper Pizazz™:** green stripe, green chevrons (*Soft Tints*)
- **specialty Paper Pizazz™:** garden (*Painted Vellum Papers #2*)
- **solid Paper Pizazz™:** white (*Plain Pastels*)
- **designer:** Arlene Peterson

Special moments in my garden.

May 2001

Use a sheet of painted vellum to accent your album pages. The tawny tones of autumn and torn paper needed only the addition of painted vellum leaves to make this page as mellow as an October afternoon. Arlene chose solid colors to harmonize with the painted vellum leaves. To create the torn paper mats, Arlene says measure the width and mark with pencil on the back of your paper, then tear the strips. Glue the torn strips together and then tear the outside edges and mat on black. She overlapped her mats on a 12"x12" sheet of gold/brown/rust plaid. The vellum leaves form a wonderful border overlapping the photo and drifting down the mat.

- **patterned Paper Pizazz™:** gold/brown/rust plaid (by the sheet)
- **specialty Paper Pizazz™:** autumn leaves (*Painted Vellum Papers #2*)
- **solid Paper Pizazz™:** black, brown, green, rust (*Solid Jewel Tones*)
- **designer:** Arlene Peterson

Tanya Fall 2000

More clever cutting of an 8¹/₂"x11" sheet of painted vellum on a 12"x12" page. Arlene trimmed the yellow rose paper to 8⁵/₈"x11¹/₄" before matting it on black and centering it on the yellow stripe. She matted the photo on black and centered it on the rose patterned paper. Using the scraps trimmed from the rose paper, she cut two ³/₄"x8¹/₄" strips, matted them on black and positioned them on both sides of the rose mat. Using one sheet of painted vellum bees, she cut the border out and placed it over the rose paper to create a frame. She used a second sheet of bees and cut out two strips with bees to place on top of the side border strips. She then cut the remaining bees from the vellum and allowed them to swarm along the photo edge. Definitely one honey of a page!

- **patterned Paper Pizazz™:** yellow stripes (*Soft Florals & Patterns*); yellow roses (*Soft Florals & Patterns,* also by the sheet)
- **specialty Paper Pizazz™:** bumble bees (*Painted Vellum,* also by the sheet)
- **solid Paper Pizazz™:** black (*Solid Jewel Tones*)
- **designer:** Arlene Peterson

Painted vellum makes it a breeze to put this page together. Arlene tore solid blue paper and sandstone patterned paper, layering them over the clouds patterned paper to create the beachside background. She cropped two photos into ovals, then matted on blue and placed them on the background. She journaled right on the shell vellum paper before gluing it over the background. Pulling colors from Alyshia's top, she matted the photo on pink with a torn paper blue mat. The photo was centered on top of the vellum. Arlene recommends printing your computer journaling on plain paper until you have it lined up where you want it before printing the vellum.

- **patterned Paper Pizazz™:** sandstone (by the sheet); clouds (*Vacation,* also by the sheet)
- **specialty Paper Pizazz™:** seashells (*Painted Vellum Papers,* also by the sheet)
- **solid Paper Pizazz™:** blue, pink (*Plain Brights*)
- **designer:** Arlene Peterson

This way…that way…up…down! Painted vellum paper doesn't always have to work on the square. Arlene turned this sheet right on its head! She created the background by trimming a sheet of soft sunflowers to 10" square and matting it on black before placing it on a 12"x12" yellow diamonds background paper. With the painted vellum sunflowers, she cut the sheet on the diagonal with the sunflowers in the corner and then trimmed around the other sunflowers. She cut a $4^1/2$" square black mat and glued a $1/2$" wide vellum mat under it. She glued the painted vellum sunflowers as shown and placed the cream matted photo under the edges of the sunflowers and glued them down. Side borders are $1/8$" wide black satin ribbon. A sheer black bow and butterflies cut from the trimmed background paper finish this sunny side up page.

- **patterned Paper Pizazz™:** yellow diamond, sunflowers (*Soft Florals & Patterns*)
- **specialty Paper Pizazz™:** sunflower vellum (*Vellum Collection*)
- **solid Paper Pizazz™:** cream (*Plain Pastels*); black (*Solid Jewel Tones*)
- **24" of $1/8$" wide black satin, 9" of $3/8$" wide sheer black ribbon:** C.M. Offray & Son, Inc.
- **black pen:** Pentel Gel Roller
- **designer:** Arlene Peterson

Arlene gets this sheet of painted vellum to work double time by making it a mat and an embellishment. She began with a 12"x12" green suede background. She angled $8^1/2$"x11" sheets of plain black and pink vellum over the green and trimmed the corners. After matting the photo on burgundy, she matted it on pink vellum leaving a $5/8$" border. A $10^3/4$"x$8^1/4$" sheet of burgundy suede was matted on black and centered on the page. Arlene trimmed $1/2$" off the right edge of the painted vellum. She trimmed around the pansy and fern images and placed it as a mat. She positioned the photo and then used the trimmed roses as an embellishment. She used the trimmed pink vellum corners for the journaling blocks. A beautiful "scrap" book page!

- **patterned Paper Pizazz™:** forest green suede, burgundy suede (by the sheet)
- **specialty Paper Pizazz™:** vellum florals and ferns (*Heritage Vellum*, also by the sheet); pink vellum (*Pastel Vellum*)
- **solid Paper Pizazz™:** black, burgundy (*Solid Jewel Tones*)
- **black pen:** Zig®Writer
- **designer:** Arlene Peterson

One of the beautiful traits of painted vellum is the way it melds with the background for new effects. Shauna cut the purple flower vellum borders off the paper and then cut them apart before placing them on both edges of the 12"x12" purple moiré background paper. After matting the photo on white and centering it on the page, she cut 1³/4" squares from lavender vellum, plum pink vellum and grass paper. Cutting the lavender vellum and grass paper squares on the diagonal for triangles, she echoed the quilt effect of the vellum border. She completed this page with white pen "stitching" and purple flower embellishments. It makes you think of twilight time in the garden. Just delicious, Shauna.

- **patterned Paper Pizazz™:** grass (by the sheet); purple moiré (*Very Pretty Papers*); purple flowers (*Embellishments*)
- **specialty Paper Pizazz™:** quilt block border vellum, quilt block border companion vellum (*Painted Vellum Papers #2*); plum pink vellum, lavender vellum (*Pastel Vellum Papers*)
- **solid Paper Pizazz™:** white (*Plain Pastels*)
- **1³/4" square punch:** Marvy® Uchida
- **black pen:** Sakura Gelly Roll
- **white pen:** Pentel Milky Gel Roller
- **designer:** Shauna Berglund-Immel

Sugar plums dance through sleepy heads in this holiday page. Shauna chose a star studded dark blue paper reminiscent of an night sky for the background. She cut 5¹/2"x8¹/2" rectangles of the brick wall paper and Christmas stocking painted vellum. She glued the sides and bottom of the vellum to the brick then cut a strip of bricks from the remaining paper and glued it at the top over the vellum. Matching and gluing the bottom and sides, she glued the vellum covered brick over the starry background. The photo, matted on red then white, and the "Santa" letter journal plaque were tucked into the pocket with care. Santa's elves everywhere are going to love doing this page!

- **patterned Paper Pizazz™:** blue stars (*Birthday Time*, also by the sheet); brick wall (by the sheet)
- **specialty Paper Pizazz™:** Christmas stocking vellum (*Painted Vellum Papers #2*)
- **solid Paper Pizazz™:** red (*Plain Brights*); white (*Plain Pastels*)
- **black pen:** Sakura Gelly Roll
- **designer:** Shauna Berglund-Immel

The pale hues of dawn, the soft shades of dusk, spring's newborn tints—pastel vellum brings a gentle wash of color to your pages. Alone or layered, in backgrounds or embellishments, you'll find so many ways to give your pages just the light touch with our pastel vellums.

A general rule for layering vellums is to place the darker shaded vellums over the lighter shades. This allows a lovely build-up of color as shown with the four shades of vellum Susan uses in this page. She begins with the pink vellum, adds the plum pink, then lavender and finally blue lavender. Each layering deepens and enriches the color of the previous layer. Outlining the layers in silver pen helps define each one and is a delicate touch in keeping with the translucency of the vellums. Doesn't this page make you think of a violet strewn April day?

- **patterned Paper Pizazz™:** lavender stripe, lavender flowers/flourishes (*Mixing Soft Patterned Papers*)
- **specialty Paper Pizazz™:** lavender vellum, blue lavender vellum, plum pink vellum (*12"x12" Pastel Vellum Papers*); pink vellum (*12"x12" Pastel Vellum Papers,* also by the sheet)
- **solid Paper Pizazz™:** white, lavender (*Plain Pastels*)
- **silver pen:** Sakura Gelly Roll
- **designer:** Susan Cobb

Beauties flourish on this page from the first place winner of the Spring Pages with Pizazz™ Contest. Kimberly Llorens began with a lavender stripe background paper. She centered an 8¹/₂"x9" sheet of lavender dot paper on top and layered lavender paper over it for a soft background that captures the girls' dresses. The photos were matted on lavender and green swirl paper with the journaling banners plain vellum over purple paper. Folded vellum "tulips" with their scattering of leaves arranged along a purple strip is just the right finishing touch. Do we know how to pick 'em! Banner patterns are on page 142. Flower folding pattern on page 140.

- **patterned Paper Pizazz™:** lavender dot (*Soft Tints*); green swirls (*Soft Tints,* also by the sheet); lavender stripe (*Soft Florals & Patterns*)
- **specialty Paper Pizazz™:** plum pink vellum, yellow lavender vellum (*Pastel Vellum Papers*); plain vellum (*Vellum Papers*)
- **solid Paper Pizazz™:** lavender vellum (*Plain Pastels*); purple (*Solid Jewel Tones*); green *Solid Muted Colors*)
- **designer:** Kimberly Llorens

WINNER

Layers of vellum can provide a feeling of delicacy to your page. See how LeNae's use of vellum highlights the tender vulnerability of Kaeley. A sheet of vellum dots covers the rose background paper muting the pattern. Two sheets of pastel vellum float over the center of the page. The layering intensifies the color behind the photo creating a rich backdrop for the black and white photo. Lacy vellum borders gently finish the layout. A page as soft as a butterfly kiss.

- **patterned Paper Pizazz™:** muted roses (by the sheet)
- **specialty Paper Pizazz™:** vellum dots (*Vellum Papers*, also by the sheet); pink, peach vellum (*Pastel Vellum*)
- **solid Paper Pizazz™:** white (*Plain Pastels*)
- **Paper Pizazz™ Cut-Outs™:** white floral borders (*Lacy Vellum*)
- **mini antique Victorian scissors:** Family Treasures, Inc.
- **white pen:** Pentel Milky Gel Roller
- **designer:** LeNae Gerig

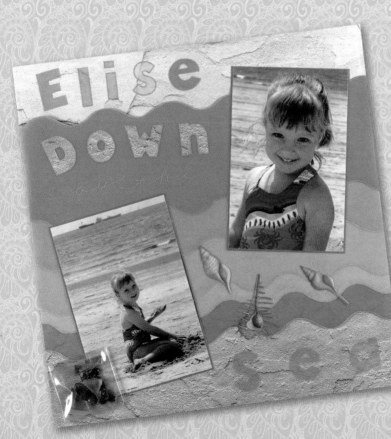

Glorious waves of vellum roll in on this wonderful seaside page. Following the colors in Elise's swimsuit, sea-hues of vellum were layered in a tidal wave of color washing over the sandstone background paper. Gold matting and pen work gleam like reflected sun as vellum cut-out shells tumble on the waves. A 2" clear memorabilia pocket holds sea glass, a souvenir of this treasured memory.

- **patterned Paper Pizazz™:** sandstone (available by the sheet)
- **specialty Paper Pizazz™:** aqua vellum, baby blue vellum, lemon vellum, sky blue vellum, lavender vellum (*12"x12" Pastel Vellum Papers*); gold (*Metallic Papers*, also by the sheet)
- **Paper Pizazz™ Cut-Outs™:** shells (*Vellum Cut-Outs™*)
- **Border Buddy™ wavy border:** EK Success Ltd
- **ABC Tracers™ template:** EK Success Ltd.
- **2" memorabilia pocket:** 3L
- **sea glass:** Sea Glass, Inc.
- **gold pen:** Pentel Hybrid Gel Roller
- **designer:** Shauna Berglund-Immel

Arlene was square on when she was inspired by Kristin's peach check rompers and satin bows. She placed 4³/8"x4¹/2" peach vellum rectangles on a 10" ivory square. Then placed a peach floral over it before gluing it to a peach check background paper. She created a breezy frame with 1" vellum squares punched and strung on a satin ribbon, glued around the photo and finished with a bow. The secret to keeping the vellum squares light and free is to glue the ribbon to the paper at the corners and in the middle of each side. The bottom border echoes the vellum frame. This is one peachy-keen page, Arlene!

- **patterned Paper Pizazz™:** peach checks (*Soft Florals & Patterns*); peach roses (*Soft Florals & Patterns,* also by the sheet)
- **specialty Paper Pizazz™:** yellow, green, peach vellum (*Pastel Vellum Papers*)
- **solid Paper Pizazz™:** cream (*Solid Pastel Papers*)
- **¹/8" hole punch:** Fiskars®, Inc.
- **¹/8" wide peach stain ribbon:** C.M. Offray & Son, Inc.
- **designer:** Arlene Peterson

Pastel vellum wraps the heritage photo in this page in a delicate photo jacket. Arlene cut a 12"x6" piece of pink vellum paper and folded 4" from each narrow end to meet in the middle. She cut a window 1¹/2" from the top and bottom and 1" from each side. Holes were punched ¹/4" down and ¹/2" from each side. The photo was matted on white and placed so Janie is centered in the jacket window. White satin bows tie the jacket closed while tiny punched butterflies embellish it delicately. Soft remembrances.

- **patterned Paper Pizazz™:** hydrangea, lavender dot (*Soft Florals & Patterns*)
- **specialty Paper Pizazz™:** pink vellum (*12"x12" Pastel Vellum Papers,* also by the sheet)
- **solid Paper Pizazz™:** white (*Plain Pastels*)
- **¹/4" wide butterfly, 1" wide flower punches:** Marvy® Uchida
- **¹/4" wide flower punch:** All Night Media®, Inc.
- **¹/2" wide butterfly punch:** Family Treasures, Inc.
- **¹/8" hole punch:** Marvy® Uchida
- **12" of ¹/8" wide white satin ribbon:** C.M. Offray & Son, Inc.
- **designer:** Arlene Peterson

When Shauna wanted to reflect the flavor of a tropical vacation, she went with cool simplicity. She chose a mosaic background paper in colors reminiscent of warm waters and balmy twilights. She matted the photo on silver and placed it centered on the background paper. She punched 1³/₄" squares from pastel vellums and outlined each with silver pen. She arranged the squares around the edges of the background paper and used silver eyelets to hold them in place. She punched ¹/₂" squares from the same colors and glued them around the photo using eyelets in the corners. In keeping it simple, Shauna journaled right on the squares. A wonderful watery page!

- **patterned Paper Pizazz™:** blue/purple/green mosaic (*Great Backgrounds*)
- **specialty Paper Pizazz™:** green vellum, lavender vellum, violet blue vellum, sky blue vellum (*Pastel Vellum Papers*); silver (*Pearlescent Papers*, also by the sheet)
- **1¹/₄" and ³/₄" wide square punches:** Marvy® Uchida
- **silver eyelets:** Stamp Studio
- **silver pen:** Pentel Hybrid Gel Roller
- **black pen:** Sakura Gelly Roll
- **designer:** Shauna Berglund-Immel

Susan created a new background by layering pastel vellum into a lovely plaid. She began with a 12"x12" sheet of yellow squiggle paper. She then cut 1" and 2" wide strips from all seven pastel vellums cutting uneven, wavy edges. She glued seven strips vertically across the paper and then six strips horizontally, varying the colors. She then added a ³/₄"x12" strip of coral in the center of one yellow horizontal and one peach vertical 2" wide strip. She matted the photos on pale yellow and dark peach. She cut a 3" square, matted it on coral vellum and glued it on point for the journaling block. The flowers were punched from pale yellow paper with yellow and coral vellum flowers glued on top. She added ¹/₄" pale yellow centers finished with pen work swirls. A sunlit beauty of a page, Susan!

- **patterned Paper Pizazz™:** yellow squiggle (*12"x12" Soft Tints*)
- **specialty Paper Pizazz™:** coral, lemon, butter, sage, mint, pale green vellums (*12"x12" Pastel Vellum Papers*); peach (*12"x12" Pastel Vellum Papers*, also by the sheet)
- **solid Paper Pizazz™:** pale yellow (*Plain Pastels*); dark peach (*Solid Muted Tones*)
- **1" wide flower punch:** Family Treasures, Inc.
- **¹/₄" wide circle punch:** McGill, Inc.
- **black pen:** Zig® Writer
- **designer:** Susan Cobb

Tone-on-tone vellums are beautiful vellum patterns created by using shades of the background color. You'll find two kinds of tone-on-tone vellum. One is white ink printed in a pattern over an uncolored vellum sheet or a darker ink color (say medium pink) over a pastel vellum sheet (perhaps light pink). Whatever tone-on-tone vellum you select, you'll find wonderful uses for these very special vellums.

It's back to the future when vellum overlays a modern paper and makes it just right for heritage photos. LeNae chose the theme-matching basketball paper for the background but it was too bright for the sepia toned heritage photos. The vellum dot overlay adds a "faded" look to the paper that makes it work perfectly. Look at the clever "mat" around the journaling plaque and the edge of the page. She cut the vellum $3/8$" larger than the journal oval and $1/4$" smaller than the background paper, allowing it to form the mat. A perfect shot!

- **patterned Paper Pizazz™:** basketballs (*Sports*, also by the sheet)
- **specialty Paper Pizazz™:** vellum dots (*Vellum Papers*, also by the sheet)
- **solid Paper Pizazz™:** brown, black (*Solid Jewel Tones*); ivory (*Plain Pastels*)
- **deckle scissors:** Family Treasures, Inc.
- **black pen:** Zig® Writer
- **designer:** LeNae Gerig

Arlene has given us a perfect example of growing a page using an $8^1/2$"x11" sheet on a 12"x12" page. She began with the fuschia plaid background paper catching the colors and pattern of Kathy's little sundress. A white-on-white vellum paper full of posies was the perfect overlay for the triple matted photo. White ribbons border the page for a sweet little girl touch. Purple vellum dragonflies Cut-Outs™ fly off the front of Kathy's dress to lead the way in this warm summer page.

- **patterned Paper Pizazz™:** fuschia plaid (by the sheet)
- **specialty Paper Pizazz™:** flower & dots vellum (*Vellum Papers*, also by the sheet)
- **solid Paper Pizazz™:** white (*Plain Pastels*); purple (*Solid Jewel Tones*)
- **Paper Pizazz™ Cut-Outs™:** dragonflies (*Vellum Cut-Outs™*)
- **scallop scissors:** Fiskars®, Inc.
- **$7/8$" white satin ribbon:** C.M. Offray & Son, Inc.
- **designer:** Arlene Peterson

LeNae ripped right into designing this page. She tore two pieces of paper from the straight edge of the white paper and glued them to the bottom of the cream sheet to form snowdrifts. She then tore out the snowman pieces and built him in the corner of the page. LeNae says to lightly trace the pattern on the back of your paper and then tear out the pieces. Chalking helped to give the snowman dimension. A sheet of snowflakes vellum was placed over the page before the photo, matted on off-white, brown tile and white, was glued to the right of the snowman. Cream and white punched snowflakes fall gently over the page. What a perfect touch the vellum gives to this winter warm page.

- **patterned Paper Pizazz™:** gold tiles (*Making Heritage Scrapbook Pages*, also by the sheet)
- **specialty Paper Pizazz™:** snowflakes vellum (*Vellum Papers*)
- **solid Paper Pizazz™:** white, off white, cream (*Plain Pastels*); orange (*Solid Muted Colors*)
- **1¹/₄" snowflake punch:** Family Treasures, Inc.
- **brown, pink decorative chalks:** Craf-T Products
- **deckle scissors:** Family Treasures, Inc.
- **black pen:** Zig® Millenium
- **foam mounting tape:** Scotch® Brand
- **designer:** LeNae Gerig

You can crimp it, stitch it, and punch it. How versatile white-on-white vellum can be! Arlene cut 1¹/₂"x12" borders and crimped them. She punched stars from each corner where the strips overlapped and then stitched the borders to the purple swirl background paper with purple embroidery floss. The photo was matted on white and purple and then placed on a 5³/₄"x6³/₄" crimped mat. Stars were punched around the mat before it was centered on the background. The punched stars were stitched with embroidery floss. Using glue dots with the punched stars and rhinestones gives a 3-D effect to the page.

- **patterned Paper Pizazz™:** purple swirl (*Great Backgrounds*)
- **specialty Paper Pizazz™:** white tri-dot vellum (*Vellum Collection*, also by the sheet)
- **solid Paper Pizazz™:** white (*Plain Pastels*); purple (*Solid Jewel Tones*)
- **¹/₂" and 1" star punches:** McGill, Inc.
- **four 12mm purple, two 8mm white rhinestones:** Creative Expressions
- **purple embroidery floss:** Coats & Clark
- **paper crimper:** Marvy® Uchida
- **glue dots:** Glue Dots International, LLC
- **designer:** Arlene Peterson

When this couple chose a rustic anniversary celebration, LeNae created a page to match. She tore rectangles of coordinating patterned papers. She matted the photo on black and then on a barnwood rectangle to match the background. She cut out white-on-white vellum dot paper the size of the photo and tore out the center to make a frame. She used the white-on-white vellum for the journaling heart, star and block then "stitched" them with pen strokes. The vellum adds lightness to the page. When tearing vellum, LeNae says, lightly draw in pencil an outline of the shape you desire, then place the vellum on a cutting surface and use the X-acto® knife to cut an "X" inside the area to be torn. Use your fingers as a guide and make very small tears as you work around your design.

- **patterned Paper Pizazz™**: barnwood, burlap (*Country*, also by the sheet); brown suede (*Black & White Photos*, also by the sheet); cedar sprigs (*"Handmade"* papers)
- **specialty Paper Pizazz™**: vellum dots (*Vellum Papers*, also by the sheet)
- **solid Paper Pizazz™**: black (*Solid Jewel Tones*)
- **deckle scissors**: Family Treasures, Inc.
- **X-acto® knife, cutting surface**: Hunt Mfg.
- **black pen**: Zig® Writer
- **designer**: LeNae Gerig

Maybe you wish the Lacy vellum design you love had a bit of color. Amy grants your wish by showing how easy it is to use chalks to get the look you want. She chalked the dandelions and leaves on the front of the vellum before layering this paper over a blue brush stroke background. Amy kept the matting simple and journaled right on the vellum for a page as sweet as a summer afternoon.

- **patterned Paper Pizazz™**: blue brush stroke (*Light Great Backgrounds*)
- **specialty Paper Pizazz™**: dandelions vellum (*Lacy Vellum*)
- **solid Paper Pizazz™**: white, blue (*Plain Pastels*)
- **yellow, green brown decorative chalks**: Craf-T Products
- **black pen**: Sakura Gelly Roll
- **designer**: Amy Gustafson

Your choice of background papers influences the look and mood of your page. Susan shows how two different background papers gives contrast to two tone-on-tone vellum papers. She cut the lavender floral and lavender paisley vellum sheets in half diagonally and placed a triangle of each on the pink satin paper to form the background. She cut 4$^1/_2$" squares from each vellum and glued each square to the pink satin before cutting them in half diagonally. She overlapped the resulting triangles onto a 6$^3/_4$"x8$^1/_4$" piece of lavender vellum. The photo was matted on white, then silver. The corners were folded from lavender vellum paper. Silver pen work was used to accent the edges of the triangles, the photo corners and for journaling. The beauty of the tone-on-tone vellum stands out.

- **patterned Paper Pizazz™:** pink moiré, pink satin (by the sheet)
- **specialty Paper Pizazz™:** lavender floral vellum, lavender paisley vellum (*Tone-On-Tone Vellum*); lavender vellum (*Pastel Vellum Papers*); metallic silver (*Metallic Papers*)
- **solid Paper Pizazz™:** white (*Plain Pastels*)
- **10" of ¼" wide lavender satin ribbon:** C.M. Offray & Son, Inc.
- **silver pen:** Sakura Gelly Roll
- **designer:** Susan Cobb

Susan created a rich look to this heritage page by layering three vellums over a yellow stripe. First a tan flourishes vellum covers the yellow stripe. Then 2"x11" strips are cut from the tan paisley vellum. Two are placed 1$^1/_2$" from each long edge—two are cut to 8$^1/_2$" long and one goes at the top and one at the bottom. A 7$^3/_4$" square of tan vellum was cut in half diagonally and placed on each side, points overlapping the center. This was repeated with 3$^1/_2$" tan vellum square and 2" tan floral vellum squares. The photo was matted on gold and ivory and attached with gold photo corners. The gold matted journaling block was slipped under the bottom vellum strip and all the edges outlined with gold pen. A golden memory.

- **patterned Paper Pizazz™:** yellow stripe (*Soft Tints*)
- **specialty Paper Pizazz™:** tan floral vellum, tan flourishes vellum (*Tone-On-Tone Vellum*); tan vellum (*12"x12" Pastel Vellum Papers;* also by the sheet); metallic gold (*Metallic Papers*, also by the sheet)
- **solid Paper Pizazz™:** ivory (*Plain Pastels*)
- **gold photo corners:** Canson-Talens, Inc.
- **gold pen:** Pentel Hybrid Gel Roller
- **designer:** Susan Cobb

Vellum may be delicate looking but it can carry its weight in color! Look at the vibrant tones! The dramatic patterns! These are the papers to give your pages the flair and pizazz of a superstar. Red carpet, please!

Richly colored vellums can give a bold swash of color without overpowering your page. In this marvelous page, Arlene began with a 8½"x11" leaf border green vellum sheet. She folded the left end to the right 3½" and then 1¼" back. She cut a 6¾" square of gold and used pattern-edged scissors on one side. She slipped the gold under the fold of the green vellum and punched ¼" holes 3¼" from each end. She tied the paper with raffia and glued it in the left corner of the page. She matted the photo on green trimmed with patterned-edged scissors and glued it centered on the gold. She cut two 1½"x11" strips of green leaf vellum paper and formed a border. Gold leaf punches float on the borders while a gold leaf die-cut matted on green serves as the journaling block. A page with a beautiful view.

- **patterned Paper Pizazz™**: sponged gold with stars (*Spattered, Crackled, Sponged*)
- **specialty Paper Pizazz™**: specialty gold (*Metallic Papers*, also by the sheet); green leaf vellum, green leaf border vellum (*Colored Vellum Papers*)
- **solid Paper Pizazz™**: green (*Solid Jewel Tones*)
- **½" and ¾" leaf punches**: Marvy® Uchida
- **¼" hole punch**: Fiskars®, Inc.
- **leaf die-cut**: Accu/Cut® Systems
- **jumbo lace scallop scissors**: Family Treasures, Inc.
- **natural raffia**: American Oak Preserving Co., Inc.
- **designer**: Arlene Peterson

Colored vellum creates a soft harmony, deepening and enriching the purple sponged background on this page. Shauna cut a 8½"x6¼" piece of purple lace border vellum and layered it over the lower part of the background paper. She used eyelets to attach the vellum—placing them in the center of the lacy circles, making them a natural part of the design. She matted the photo on lavender and tucked it in the pocket with a note written on lavender matted on white paper. Shauna reversed the colors for the journaling block. Lacy vellum butterfly cut-outs and a sheer bow complete this "love is in the air" page.

- **patterned Paper Pizazz™**: purple sponged (*Pretty Papers*, also by the sheet)
- **specialty Paper Pizazz™**: purple lace vellum (*Colored Vellum Papers*); baby blue vellum (*Pastel Vellum Papers*)
- **solid Paper Pizazz™**: lavender, white (*Plain Pastels*)
- **Paper Pizazz™ Cut-Outs™**: butterflies (*Lacy Vellum Cut-Outs™*)
- **white eyelets**: AmericanPin/HyGlo
- **10" of ⅞" wide sheer lavender ribbon**: C.M. Offray & Son, Inc.
- **blue pen**: Zig® Writer
- **designer**: Shauna Berglund-Immel

Snow pictures are wonderful but they're so…well, basic white. Arlene says to build a great page toss in some bright colors. She began with a clouds background paper and then added 4^{1}/$_{4}$"x5^{1}/$_{2}$" rectangles of blue vellum with snowflakes in opposite corners. Going with Scott's bright red hat, she matted the pictures on red, then blue vellum snowflakes, white and red. By matting the pictures together and using quadruple matting, she adds to their focus. Red and white letters and journaling blocks finish this fun page. What a great way to play in the snow and still stay warm!

- **patterned Paper Pizazz™:** clouds (*Vacation*, also by the sheet)
- **specialty Paper Pizazz™:** blue vellum with snowflakes (by the sheet)
- **solid Paper Pizazz™:** white (*Plain Pastels*); red (*Plain Brights*)
- **1^{1}/$_{4}$" traveler letter die-cuts:** Accu/Cut® Systems
- **designer:** Arlene Peterson

Watch how Arlene takes one beautiful sheet of 8^{1}/$_{2}$"x11" colored vellum and and grows it into a whole 12"x12" page of beautiful tone-on-tone ideas. She began with purple squares border vellum. She cut the border off, divided it into two sections and glued it on the 12"x12" "handmade" purple background for a new border. The small photos were matted first on white and then on purple stitch vellum. The center photo was matted like the smaller ones then again on the cut-out center of the border vellum. The vellum mats were outlined in white pen. Light purple photos corners add a charming touch to this page. A lifetime of memories beautifully preserved.

- **patterned Paper Pizazz™:** purple "handmade" (*The "Handmade" Look*)
- **specialty Paper Pizazz™:** purple squares border vellum, purple stitch vellum (*Colored Vellum Papers*)
- **solid Paper Pizazz™:** white (*Plain Pastels*)
- **purple photo corners:** Canson-Talens, Inc.
- **white pen:** Pentel Milky Gel Roller
- **designer:** Arlene Peterson

This lively page is the perfect stage for these two brightly dressed dancers! Shauna chose a blue stripe with green dots background paper that matched the clothing. She layered a 5¹/₂"x11" piece of green checked vellum over the center of the paper. The photo was matted on white trimmed with patterned edged scissors. A floral border was attached ¹/₂" from the top with eyelets as the flower centers. A green checked button was attached to the center of the flower cut-out with embroidery thread. Another flower popped up on foam mounting tape in the corner of the photo. A rockin' page, Shauna!

- **patterned Paper Pizazz™:** blue stripes with green dots (*A Girl's Scrapbook*)
- **specialty Paper Pizazz™:** green checks vellum (*Colored Vellum Papers*)
- **solid Paper Pizazz™:** white (*Plain Pastels*)
- **Paper Pizazz™ Cut-Outs™:** floral border, flowers (*A Girl's Scrapbook*)
- **white eyelets:** Stamp Studio
- **³/₄" green checked button:** Jesse James Button & Trim
- **turquoise blue embroidery floss:** DMC Corp.
- **mini scallop scissors:** Fiskars®, Inc.
- **blue pen:** Zig® Writer
- **designer:** Shauna Berglund-Immel

Colored vellum is the key to making this very simple page look so special. Shauna chose sponged leaves for the background paper. She die-cut two leaves out of a 4"x11" strip of green leaves colored vellum and outlined them with gold pen. She attached the vellum with gold brads. She then stitched the left edge of the vellum with gold thread. The photo was matted first on gold and then on pale yellow outlined with gold. Shauna used two stitches in opposite corners to embellish the photo. The journaling was done directly on the page. A clean, outdoor fresh page…just right for its masculine subjects.

- **patterned Paper Pizazz™:** sponged leaves (*A Woman's Scrapbook*, also by the sheet)
- **specialty Paper Pizazz™:** green leaves vellum (*Colored Vellum Papers*); gold (*Metallic Papers*, also by the sheet)
- **solid Paper Pizazz™:** pale yellow (*Plain Pastels*)
- **maple leaf die-cut:** Ellison® Craft & Design
- **metallic gold thread:** Westrim® Crafts
- **gold brads:** AmericanPin/Hyglo
- **green pen:** Zig® Writer
- **gold pen:** Pentel Hybrid Gel Roller
- **designer:** Shauna Berglund-Immel

Shauna makes putting a page together so easy! Using the "vintage" style of the photo as the starting point, she chose an old-fashioned looking background. She then matted the photo on white, a coordinating dot and white again. Now watch how quickly she creates that extra special touch using colored vellum paper. Shauna took an 8^1/$_2$"x11" sheet of vellum corner pansies and folded it in half. She then folded the corner (with the pansies) back until the edge met the fold. She attached the pocket to the background, tucked in the photo and the added a sheer plum bow at the corner. What could be easier than 1•2•3 or more beautiful?

- **patterned Paper Pizazz™**: lacy dots, lacy floral stripes (*Lovely & Lacy Papers*)
- **specialty Paper Pizazz™**: vellum corner pansies (*Colored Vellum Papers*, also by the sheet)
- **solid Paper Pizazz™**: white (*Plain Pastels*)
- **12" of 1^1/$_2$" wide sheer plum ribbon**: C.M. Offray & Son, Inc.
- **white pen**: Pentel Milky Gel Roller
- **photography**: I.N.V.U. Portraits by Helen
- **designer**: Shauna Berglund-Immel

The wedding photo was lovely with its muted tones but when Shauna spotted the bright yellow flower in the boutonniere she knew just how to light up this page. She selected a matching yellow stitch colored 8^1/$_2$"x11" vellum and cut it into two triangles. She then cut 1^3/$_4$" squares from each corner of the triangles. She placed the vellum triangles over the corners of the 12"x12" white roses background paper and glued ^{1}/$_8$" wide white ribbon over the cut edges. The photo was matted on white and sage green then placed offset on the background. Shauna says the stitching lines on the vellum paper makes it easy to cut it correctly. A glowing moment wrapped forever in sunshine.

- **patterned Paper Pizazz™**: 12"x12" white roses (by the sheet)
- **specialty Paper Pizazz™**: stitched yellow squares vellum (*Colored Vellum Papers*)
- **solid Paper Pizazz™**: white (*Plain Pastels*); sage green (*Solid Muted Colors*)
- **40" of ^{1}/$_8$" wide white satin ribbon**: C.M. Offray & Son, Inc.
- **white pen**: Pentel Milky Gel Roller
- **designer**: Shauna Berglund-Immel

Softly patterned vellums are a sociable group. They love mixing with everything. Introduce them to patterned papers, plain papers, or plain vellums and you'll find all your elements blending into one beautiful page.

Soft patterned vellums are multi-faceted and show off their masculine side in this page! Shauna began with an aqua satin background paper matching the handkerchiefs in the pockets. She tore 4" from the right side of an aqua dot vellum sheet and "cross-stitched" it to the background with metallic silver thread. After the photo was matted on silver and aqua vellum, she stitched it onto the page along with the torn vellum journaling plaque. A ¹/₄"x11" strip of lavender checked vellum was glued ¹/₂" from the right edge and three 1" square blocks of lavender check were added. Note how Shauna cut out two adjoining squares from the checked vellum blocks and outlined all the edges with silver pen. Soft colors…strong page!

- **patterned Paper Pizazz™:** aqua satin (*Bright Great Backgrounds*)
- **specialty Paper Pizazz™:** aqua dot vellum, lavender checked vellum (*Soft Patterns in Vellum*); aqua vellum (*Pastel Vellum Papers*); silver (*Heavy Metal Papers*, also by the sheet)
- **metallic silver thread:** Coats & Clark
- **silver pen:** Pentel Hybrid Gel Roller
- **designer:** Shauna Berglund-Immel

Bargello (see page 80) is a great technique for mixing patterned vellums. Susan used a lavender striped vellum, lavender diamond vellum, and white-on-white vellum flowers along with two plain vellums to create the renaissance feel of this page. Layering 1" wide strips of vellum over a purple satin background paper sets the stage for the photo triple matted in white, pink vellum and a flower vellum matching Lauren's dress. A white matted journaling plaque and a satin ribbon provide the simple touches to finish this page perfectly.

- **patterned Paper Pizazz™:** purple satin (*Bright Great Backgrounds*, also by the sheet)
- **specialty Paper Pizazz™:** lavender stripe vellum, lavender diamonds vellum (*Soft Patterns in Vellum*); plum pink vellum (*Pastel Vellum Papers*); vellum flowers & dots (*Vellum Papers*, also by the sheet)
- **solid Paper Pizazz™:** white (*Plain Pastels*)
- **silver photo corners:** Canson-Talens, Inc.
- **small heart #2 die-cut:** Accu/Cut® Systems
- **9" of ³/₈" wide pink satin ribbon:** C.M. Offray & Son, Inc. heart #2 ©&™ Accu/Cut® Systems
- **silver pen:** Sakura Gelly Roll
- **designer:** Susan Cobb

There's magic in LeNae's method of pulling this page together. She selects her colors from the clothing in the photo and begins with a purple/lavender stripe background paper. Trimming ¹/₂" from each side of the white lace paper, she glues it centered on the page. She mats the photo on white and then a purple diamond vellum. The lace is subtle enough to allow the vellum pattern to remain crisp. She cut a 7"x4¹/₂" piece of purple stripe vellum. She trimmed the roses from the rose vellum, placed it over the striped vellum and cut a "V" following the line of the rose overlay. She slipped the matted photo under the roses, glued everything in place and abracadabra…beautiful!

- **patterned Paper Pizazz™:** purple stripe (*Soft Tints*); white lace (*Textured Papers*)
- **specialty Paper Pizazz™:** purple diamonds vellum, purple stripe vellum (*Soft Patterns in Vellum*); rose vellum (*Floral Vellum Papers*)
- **solid Paper Pizazz™:** *white (Plain Pastels)*
- **mini antique Victorian scissors:** Family Treasures, Inc.
- **lavender pen:** Pentel Milky Gel Roller
- **designer:** LeNae Gerig

The purple/pink swirls background paper could overpower the tinted photo in this page but Shauna skillfully used vellum to not only reflect the colors in the photo but to help gentle the brightness. She matted the photo on dark pink and blue lavender vellums edged with gold pen. She placed the matted photo over a 1³/₄" wide strip of the purple striped vellum centered on the background. She cut a sheet of the pink lattice to 4" wide and "pinked" the edge for interest. Using the lattice for a pattern, she cut "X"s in the vellum and folded the edges back to form squares. She used gold pen on the edges and for the journaling then layered the vellum over the left side of the background paper and the photo finishing with two vellum paper knots. Retro done right, Shauna!

- **patterned Paper Pizazz™:** pink/purple swirls (*Bright Great Backgrounds*)
- **specialty Paper Pizazz™:** specialty gold (*Metallic Papers*, also by the sheet); blue lavender vellum, dark pink vellum (*Pastel Vellum Papers*); pink lattice vellum, purple striped vellum (*Soft Patterns in Vellum*)
- **gold pen:** Pentel Hybrid Gel Roller
- **designer:** Shauna Berglund-Immel

Nothing is richer than the look of gold! Nothing else can give such marvelous opulence to any page. The secret is to begin with a simple layout. Now add the metallic vellum. Voila! With the magic of gold, your page becomes a true treasure.

Darn! Everyone was having such a good time they forgot to take many pictures! If this ever happens at a big family event, Shauna shows you how to preserve the day beautifully anyway. She began this Thanksgiving page by layering the elegant gold leaves vellum over a fall leaves background. A single photo is matted in gold and "handmade" paper edged with gold pen. In lieu of missing photos, Shauna lists the menu and the guest list. With the scattering of tiny gold leaves, this is a page to serve up warm memories any time.

- **patterned Paper Pizazz™:** autumn leaves (*Holidays & Seasons,* also by the sheet); green handmade (*"Handmade" Papers,* also by the sheet)
- **specialty Paper Pizazz™:** gold leaves vellum (*Metallic on Vellum*); teal vellum (*Pastel Vellum Papers*); gold (*Metallic Papers,* also by the sheet)
- **leaf punches:** Family Treasures, Inc.
- **sticky dot adhesive:** Therm O Web
- **gold pen:** Sakura Gelly Roll
- **designer:** Shauna Berglund-Immel

Watch Shauna grow one beautiful page with only one picture. She begins with a pink 12"x12" background selected to match the color and texture of Elise's pink sweater. The tulip paper is a marvelous match for the background but a bit small. To stretch and balance the page, Shaua cut the gold lace border off a metallic vellum sheet and literally stitched it to the tulip paper with pink thread for a charming "handmade" effect. The pink paper journal tag is raised with foam tape and the ends of the gold hanger slip into slits on each side of the bouquet and tied in back. Isn't this a fabulous spring page?

- **patterned Paper Pizazz™:** pink on pink (*Heritage Papers*); tulips (*Bj's Gold and Handpainted Papers*)
- **specialty Paper Pizazz™:** gold lace vellum (*Metallic on Vellum*); gold (*Metallic Papers,* also by the sheet)
- **solid Paper Pizazz™:** white, pink (*Plain Pastels*)
- **gift tag die-cut:** Accu/Cut® Systems
- **pink thread:** Coats & Clark
- **gold metallic thread:** Westrim® Crafts
- **foam mounting tape:** Scotch® Brand
- **designer:** Shauna Berglund-Immel

Metallic vellum attracts all kinds of wonderful things like the gold snowflake charms dusting this page. Shauna uses the metallic vellum border horizontally on a page then uses the remaining vellum as a mat. She began with the starry night patterned paper and trimmed it to 8½"x7½". Stringing each charm on gold thread, she glued the thread ends to the back of the starry paper and then glued the starry paper to the clouds patterned paper with a dot of glue under each charm to secure it to the paper. She cut off the metallic snowflakes border and placed it over the seam joining the two background papers. Two ⅛"x8½" strips of gold paper were glued over the edges of the vellum. The photo was mounted on gold and then the vellum trimmed from the snowflakes. Gold pen journaling completes this very cool page.

- **patterned Paper Pizazz™:** clouds (*Vacation #2*, also by the sheet); starry night (by the sheet)
- **specialty Paper Pizazz™:** metallic snowflake vellum (*Metallic on Vellum*); gold (*Metallic Papers*, also by the sheet)
- **gold snowflake charms:** 3L
- **metallic gold thread:** Coats & Clark
- **glue dots:** Glue Dots International, LLC
- **gold pen:** Pentel Milky Gel Writer
- **designer:** Shauna Berglund-Immel

Metallic vellum comes in 8½"x11" and it's the perfect accent for any size page even this 12"x12" page. Shauna chose a creamy bordered paper for the background. She matted the photo and the wedding announcement on gold then plain vellum edged with gold pen work and positioned them on the page. She trimmed a sheet of gold metallic tile vellum border to 6"x10¾" then cut a slit every ¾" through the center of the border. A gold edged white satin ribbon was woven through the slits. The double-heart charm was hung on gold thread and the loop slipped over the ribbon before it was tied in a bow. The vellum sheet was glued to form a pocket over the announcement and photo then gold pen journaling finished the page. A sweetheart of a page, Shauna.

- **patterned Paper Pizazz™:** cream with flowered border (by the sheet)
- **specialty Paper Pizazz™:** gold tile border vellum (*Metallic on Vellum*); gold (*Metallic Papers*, also by the sheet)
- **gold double-heart charm:** 3L
- **metallic gold thread:** Westrim® Crafts
- **⅛" wide white satin with gold metallic edged ribbon:** C.M. Offray & Son, Inc.
- **designer:** Shauna Berglund-Immel

The royal treatment is what this page received. A tiny queen in her realm had Shauna bring forth the purple "velvet" for her background paper with a pink satin to match her gown. The 8½"x11" metallic lace border was trimmed and glued across the top of the satin patterned paper and then crowned with "jewels". Shauna used ¼" of the edge of a second sheet of metallic gold lace to border the satin paper. She cut journaling letters from the center of the metallic vellum border and used scrap points to create gem-topped photo corners. A curtesy to our own "queen" of design.

- **patterned Paper Pizazz™:** purple "velvet" (*"Velvet" Backgrounds*); pink satin (*Very Pretty Papers*)
- **specialty Paper Pizazz™:** gold (*Metallic Papers*, also by the sheet); metallic lace border (*Metallic on Vellum*)
- **assorted rhinestones:** Crafty Expressions
- **traveller letter die-cuts:** Accu/Cut® Systems
- **gold pen:** Pentel Milky Gel Roller
- **designer:** Shauna Berglund-Immel

Shauna gives her imagination wings with this page. She layered gold metallic butterflies over a purple sponged background paper. She silhouette cut around the purple daisies 5½" from the right side. She then silhouette cut a journaling space from among the daisies and outlined all the cut edges with gold pen. The photo was matted on gold and plain vellum from the butterflies paper then the mats were outlined with gold pen. Shauna cut out two daisies, outlined the edges with gold and popped them off the page with foam mounting tape. A page to make your heart flutter!

- **patterned Paper Pizazz™:** purple sponged (*Pretty Papers*, also by the sheet); purple daisies (by the sheet)
- **specialty Paper Pizazz™:** gold (*Metallic Papers*, also by the sheet); gold metallic butterflies/ dragonflies (*Metallic on Vellum*)
- **glue dots:** Glue Dots International LLC
- **gold pen:** Pentel Hybrid Gel Roller
- **designer:** Shauna Berglund-Immel

Some pictures are so completely perfect in what they depict, less becomes more on a page. Here a beautiful bride and her handsome groom kiss in front of a glorious sunset and then stand silhouetted against the light. Shauna created an page that emphasizes the moment. She chose a cream roses background paper with colors to match both the bouquet and setting sun. The photos were matted on gold and positioned to the right side of the paper. She tore a strip of peach moiré paper the width of the gold metallic rose border and layered it over the cream roses. The vellum was cut to form frames over the photos. Gold pen journaling and a sheer gold-edged bow make this page as memorable as the moment it holds.

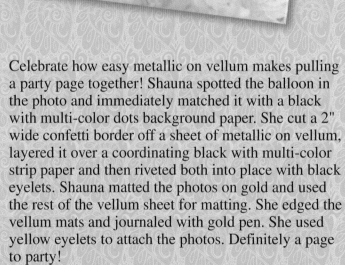

- **patterned Paper Pizazz™:** cream roses, peach moiré (*Pretty Papers*, also by the sheet)
- **specialty Paper Pizazz™:** metallic rose vellum (*Metallic Vellum Papers*); gold (*Metallic Papers*, also by the sheet)
- **⁵⁄₈" wide gold-edged sheer ribbon:** C.M. Offray & Son, Inc.
- **gold pen:** Pentel Hybrid Gel Roller
- **designer:** Shauna Berglund-Immel

Celebrate how easy metallic on vellum makes pulling a party page together! Shauna spotted the balloon in the photo and immediately matched it with a black with multi-color dots background paper. She cut a 2" wide confetti border off a sheet of metallic on vellum, layered it over a coordinating black with multi-color strip paper and then riveted both into place with black eyelets. Shauna matted the photos on gold and used the rest of the vellum sheet for matting. She edged the vellum mats and journaled with gold pen. She used yellow eyelets to attach the photos. Definitely a page to party!

- **patterned Paper Pizazz™:** black with multi-color dots, black with multi-color stripes (*Bright Great Backgrounds*)
- **specialty Paper Pizazz™:** metallic confetti vellum (*Metallic on Vellum*); gold (*Metallic Papers*, also by the sheet)
- **¹⁄₈" wide hole punch:** McGill, Inc.
- **black and yellow eyelets:** AmericanPin/HyGlo
- **gold pen:** Pentel Hybrid gel Roller
- **black pen:** Sakura Gelly Roll
- **designer:** Shauna Berglund-Immel

When a page is designed with delicate elements, many embellishments can overpower it. Accents as light as the paper are needed. Lacy Vellum Cut-Outs™ float onto your page soft as down.

Travis & Trea Engagement 2001

Lacy Vellum Cut-Outs™ can help your pages blossom and take wing! Susan started with a very simple page. First she double matted the photo and used the notch punch on the corners. Silver thread was wound around the corners and finished in a bow. The lacy vellum was trimmed to 7³/8"x10" and the inside cut ¹/8" larger than the matted photo. The blue windowpane was trimmed to match the size of the vellum. The windowpane and vellum were glued together and the photo glued in the "window" before being glued centered to the blue diamond paper. When she added the blue flowers and butterfly *Lacy Vellum Cut-Outs™*, this page soared to marvelous.

- **patterned Paper Pizazz™:** blue diamond, blue screen (*Bright Tints*)
- **specialty Paper Pizazz™:** baby blue vellum (*Pastel Vellum Papers*); vine/border vellum (*Lacy Vellum*)
- **solid Paper Pizazz™:** white (*Plain Pastels*)
- **Paper Pizazz™ Cut-Outs™:** butterfly, flowers (*Lacy Vellum Cut-Outs™*)
- **notch corner punch:** Marvy® Uchida
- **white pen:** Pentel Milky Gel Roller
- **silver thread:** Westrim® Crafts
- **designer:** Susan Cobb

Butterflies dance on this lighter than air page. Susan used the technique of layering vellum to give the effect of a number of vellum colors having been used instead of just two. She placed a 2"x6" strip of pink vellum 1¹/2" from the right edge of the paper. She then layered a 6" square of yellow on point over the strip. She layered a 6" square of pink over the yellow and then added a 3³/4"x6" butterfly border. The photo was doubled matted on pink and yellow vellum. The lacy vellum butterfly border added a charming touch but Susan wanted some butterflies to roam free on her page. Since *Lacy Vellum Cut-Outs™* provide matching elements to the *Lacy Vellum* pages, she quickly netted what she needed to finish her page. And it's a top-flight job!

- **patterned Paper Pizazz™:** pink/yellow plaid (by the sheet)
- **specialty Paper Pizazz™:** butter vellum, pink vellum (*Pastel Vellum Papers*); butterfly vellum (*Lacy Vellum*)
- **solid Paper Pizazz™:** white (*Plain Pastels*)
- **Paper Pizazz™ Cut-Outs™:** butterflies (*Lacy Vellum Cut-Outs™*)
- **white pen:** Pentel Milky Gel Roller
- **designer:** Susan Cobb

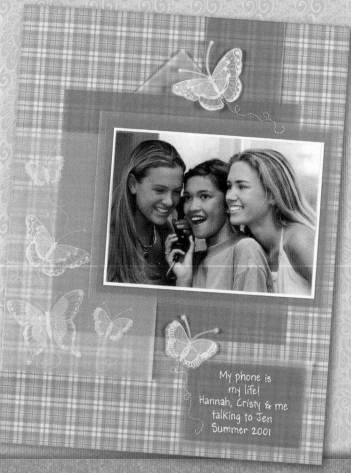

My phone is my life! Hannah, Cristy & me talking to Jen Summer 2001

Vellum Cut-Outs™ are color-drenched designs for pages yet, being vellum, they add a light touch to your page.

See the magic Shauna creates in this page with four patterned papers! Beginning with a background reminiscent of reflections on water, she ripples the edge and mats it over a green swirl background. Pulling colors out of the background she used five mats on the photo. She edged the vellum, blue tiles and green gingham borders with a silver pen, deftly unifying them with the silver matting. As the matted photo floats on its background, two vellum cut-out dragonflies add the fairy dust that turns this page into a midsummer's dream!

- **patterned Paper Pizazz™:** blue tiles, blue/multi color reflections (*Great Bright Backgrounds*); green gingham, green swirl (*Soft Tints*)
- **specialty Paper Pizazz™:** silver (by the sheet); pastel blue vellum (*Pastel Vellum Papers*)
- **Paper Pizazz™ Cut-Outs™:** dragonflies (*Vellum Cut-Outs™*)
- **original border Buddy™:** EK Success Ltd.
- **silver pen:** Zebra Jimnie Gel Rollerball
- **designer:** Shauna Berglund-Immel

The gleam of gold makes this page glow with fall splendor. Gold-touched borders illuminate the harvest theme. Matting the background on gold and centering it over a rich velvety red sets the perfect stage for the gold-edged vellum leaves drifting across it. The leaves swirl around the gold matted photo and off the background to lead your eye throughout the page. A great page for every "punkin" in your patch.

- **patterned Paper Pizazz™:** red velvet (*"Velvet" Backgrounds*); gold foiled leaf borders (*Bj's Gold and Handpainted Papers*)
- **specialty Paper Pizazz™:** gold (*Heavy Metal Papers*)
- **Paper Pizazz™ Cut-Outs™:** leaves (*Vellum Cut-Outs™*)
- **mini antique Victorian scissors:** Family Treasures, Inc.
- **gold pen:** Sakura Gelly Roll
- **evergreen pen:** Zig® Writer
- **designer:** Shauna Berglund-Immel

BASIC TRIANGLE FOLD

PATTERNS

Use 2"–3" squares for the triangle fold.

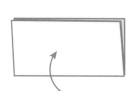

Fold the bottom of the square to meet the top edge and crease. Unfold.

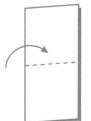

Fold the square to to the right edge and crease.

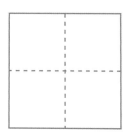

Open and turn the paper over.

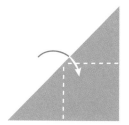

Fold the upper left corner to the bottom right corner and crease. Unfold.

Fold the bottom left corner to the upper right corner and crease. Unfold.

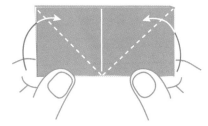

Fold the paper in half and turn as shown.

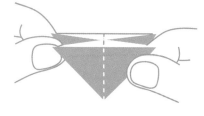

Using your fingers, push up and in the sides as shown.

Basic form.

FLOWER FOLD — PAGE 120

Fold a basic triangle from a 2¹/₂" square for each flower (see above).

Fold the top right flap to the left.

Fold the right flap down along the center line and crease.

Fold the top left flap back to the right.

Mark a place on the right flap ¹/₄ of the way up from the bottom point.

Fold the top right flap down and align edge with mark.

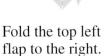

Fold the top left flap to the right.

Fold the left flap down along the center line.

Fold the right flap back to the left.

Mark a point ¹/₄ of the way from the point and fold the flap as shown.

SNOWFLAKE FOLD

— PAGE 98

Fold four basic triangles from a 3" square papers (see above). Beginning with the triangle fold, turn the triangle so the point is at the right. Cut 1" off the point.

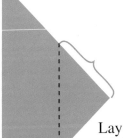

Lay two triangles parallel with the cut edges facing. With a third triangle, slip one end between the folds of the right triangle. Slip the second triangle between the folds of the third triangle as shown. Reverse and repeat for the fourth triangle.

PATTERNS

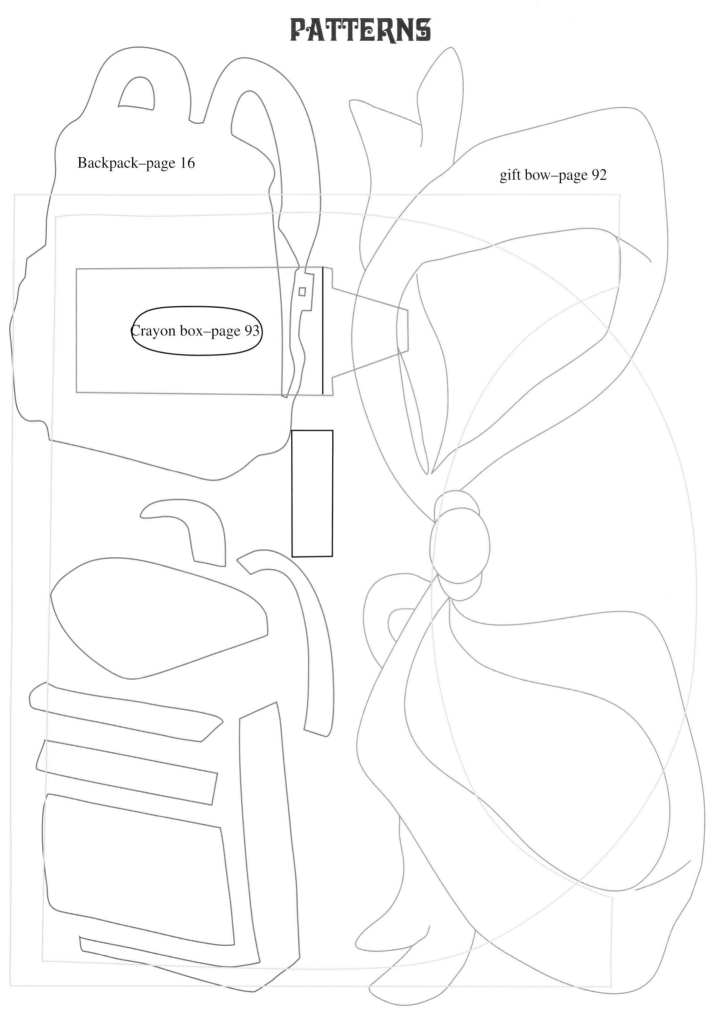

Backpack–page 16

gift bow–page 92

Crayon box–page 93

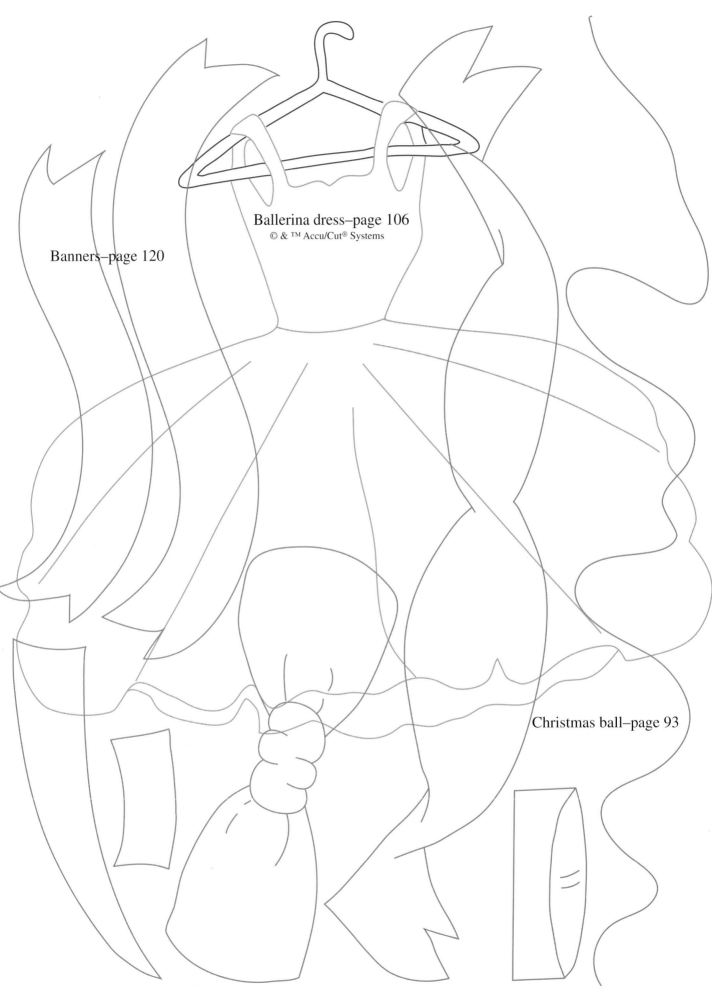

Banners–page 120

Ballerina dress–page 106
© & ™ Accu/Cut® Systems

Christmas ball–page 93

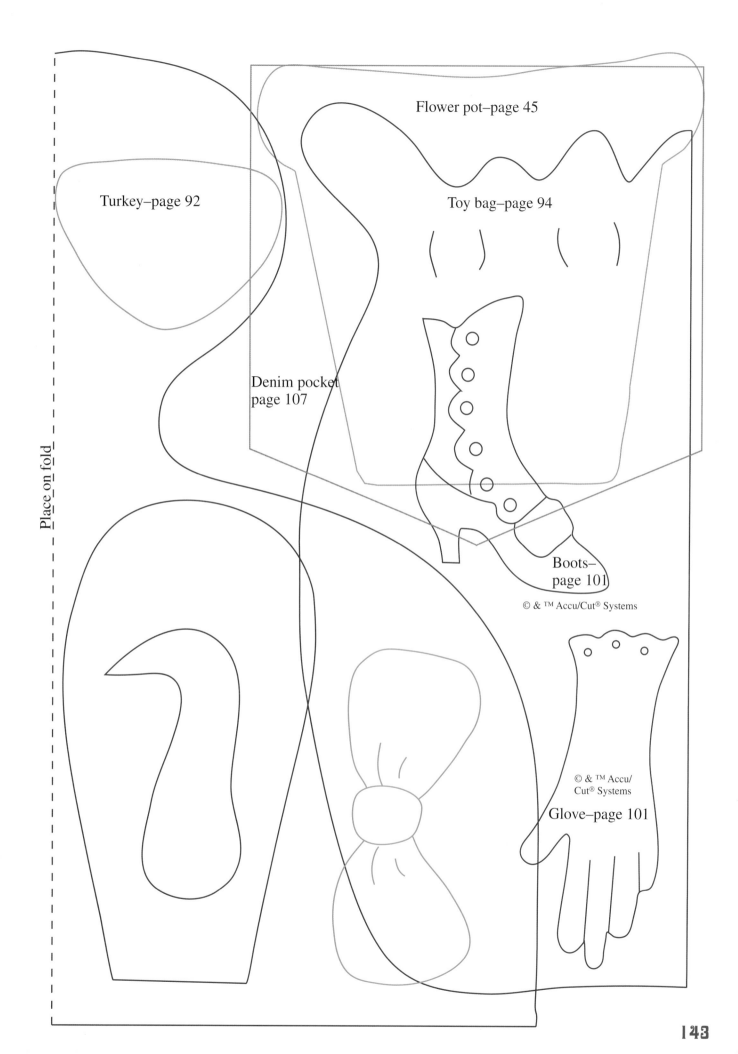

Flower pot–page 45

Turkey–page 92

Toy bag–page 94

Denim pocket
page 107

Boots–
page 101

Glove–page 101

Place on fold

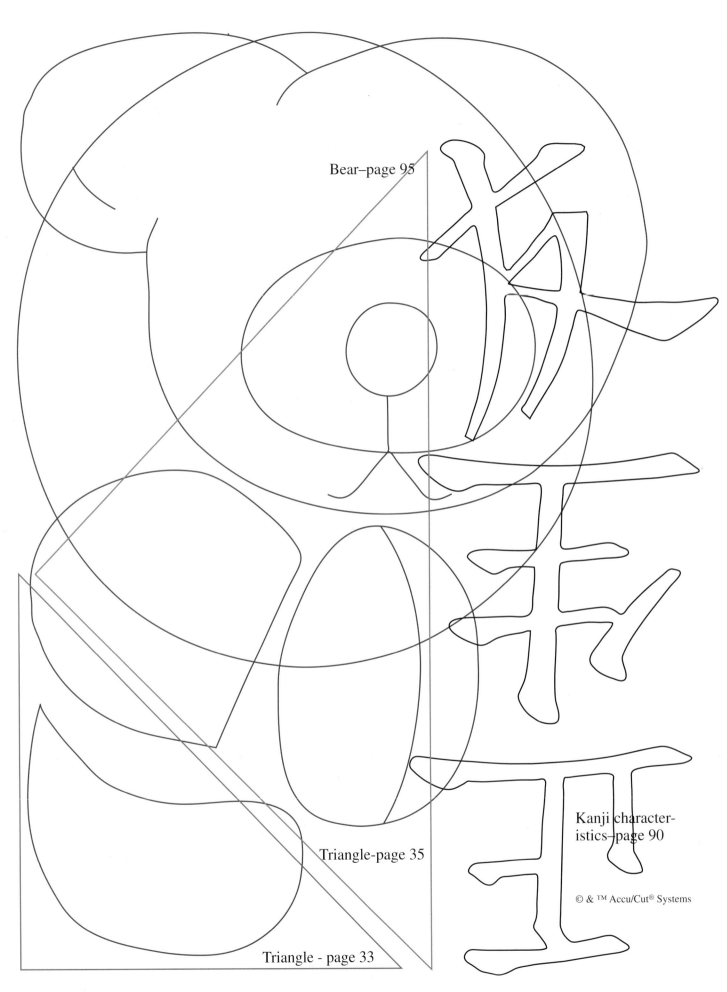

Bear–page 95

Kanji character-
istics–page 90

© & ™ Accu/Cut® Systems

Triangle-page 35

Triangle - page 33

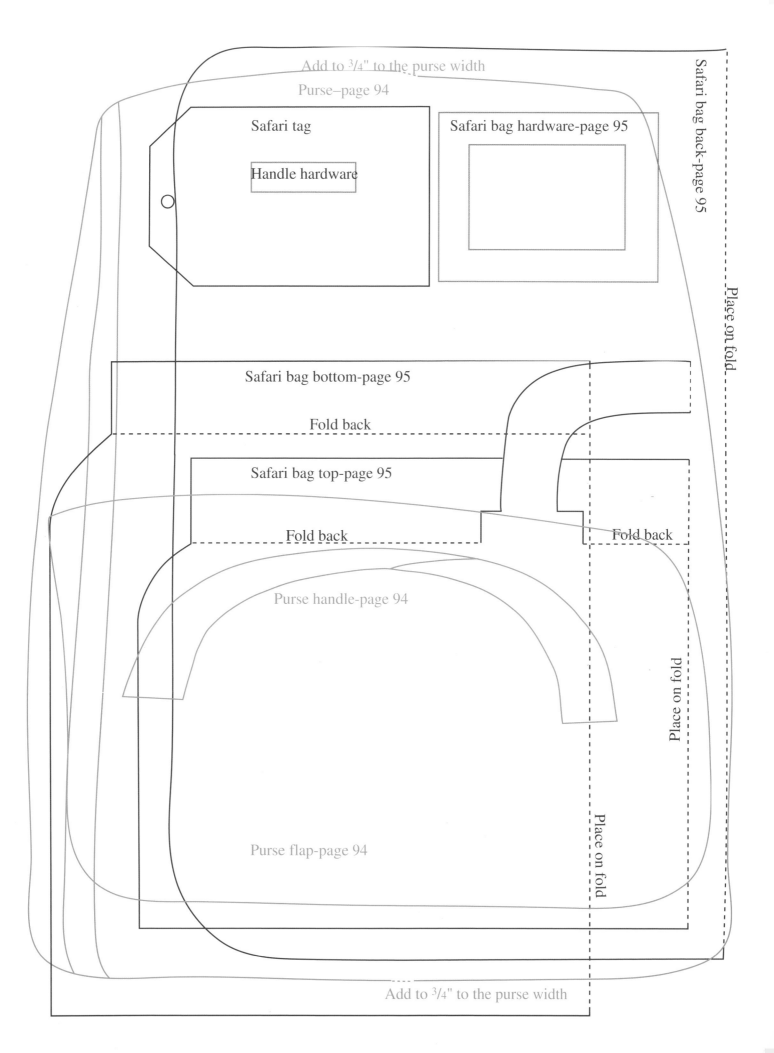

Add to ¾" to the purse width

Purse–page 94

Safari tag

Handle hardware

Safari bag hardware-page 95

Safari bag back-page 95

Place on fold

Safari bag bottom-page 95

Fold back

Safari bag top-page 95

Fold back

Fold back

Purse handle-page 94

Place on fold

Purse flap-page 94

Place on fold

Add to ¾" to the purse width

More Scrapbooking Products
from Hot Off The Press

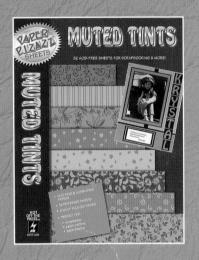

ISBN 1-56231-773-3

90000

9 781562 317737

UPC

0 35788 02275 3

www.paperpizazz.com